OVERFLOWING LIFE

OVERFLOWING LIFE

Second Edition, Revised

ROBERT C. FROST, PhD

Logos International
Plainfield, New Jersey

All quotations from Scripture are taken from the King James Version of the Holy Bible or author's paraphrase unless indicated by one of the following symbols:

JB = *Jerusalem Bible* (Garden City, New York: Doubleday, 1969)

Lasma = *The Holy Bible, translated from ancient Eastern manuscripts,* by George M. Lamsa. 5th ed. (Philadelphia, Pa.: Holman, 1961)

NEB = *The New English Bible* (New York, N.Y.: Oxford Univ. Press, 1961)

Phillips = *The New Testament in Modern English,* tr. by J. B. Phillips (New York, N.Y.: Macmillan, 1958)

TAB = *The Amplified Bible* (Grand Rapids, Mich.: Zondervan, 1965)

TLB = *The Living Bible* (Wheaton, Ill.: Tyndale House, 1971)

TLG = *The Living Gospels* (Wheaton, Ill.: Tyndale House, 1966)

various translations = compiled, in part, from *The New Testament from 26 Translations* (Grand Rapids, Mich.: Zondervan, 1967)

Weymouth = *Weymouth's New Testament in Modern Speech* (New York: Harper & Row, 1951)

Williams = *The New Testament in the Language of the People,* by Charles R. Williams (Chicago, Ill.: Moody Press, 1963)

Wuest = *The New Testament: An Expanded Translation,* by Kenneth A. Wuest (Grand Rapids, Mich.: Eerdmans, 1961)

OVERFLOWING LIFE, second edition, revised
© 1973 by Logos Internationa, Plainfield, NJ 07060
First edition © 1971
All Rights Reserved
Printed in the United States of America
Library of Congress Catalog Card Number 72-146696

ISBN Hardcover 0-88270-049-9
ISBN Paperback 0-88270-050-2

Dedicated in love and devotion

to my mother

Rose Virginia Frost

who faithfully led me

at an early age

to the

Springs of Living Water

CONTENTS

FOREWORD

The Holy Spirit is a very practical person who desires to direct the power of God into every area of our personal lives. The graces and gifts of the Spirit become streams of life by which Jesus Christ sets us free to become ourselves in Him. In this book, various aspects of our devotional life and personal ministry are discussed within a charismatic framework. The unique privileges and problems related to the Spirit-filled home and community are considered in a practical forthright fashion. The principles by which the believer can discern truth and error are presented within a Christ-centered perspective. The themes discussed are all related to personal experience in the charismatic movement which currently is reaching every area of Christendom the world over.

PREFACE TO OVERFLOWING LIFE

The chapters related to our life and walk in the Spirit in the first edition of *Aglow with the Spirit* have in this volume been increased in number and content and published under a different title. The second edition of *Aglow with the Spirit* deals with the Baptism in the Holy Spirit and forms the foundation upon which this volume is based. The two books complement each other and are designed to aid the believer in understanding his spiritual privileges and responsibilities as an earthly member of God's heavenly family.

Some seven years have elapsed since the first edition was written. Several areas of vital interest and need have become evident as time and travel both in the United States and abroad have provided the necessary opportunities for observation and evaluation. There is a growing appreciation for the true concept of Christian community within the charismatic context. As with the first community, described in the opening chapters of Acts, the life of the fellowship is related to the twofold function of unity within and witness without. In this, Christ's intercessory prayer finds its fulfillment. "Father I pray that they might be one . . . that the world might believe!" (John 17:21).

The "climax of the ages" as envisoned by the apostle Paul is now coming into view! (Eph. 1:9-11 TAB). The theme of the new edition relates to this divine desire which our Heavenly Father has conceived for His earthly family. God is yet going to have a people for His name.

The Holy Spirit is most practical, and the heavenly ideal finds its realizations as our own earthly families are claimed for God's divine purpose. Satan has intensified his attack upon the Christian family for He recognizes the power which can be generated by "two or three" truly united together in Jesus' name! For this reason a chapter on the Spirit-filled home has been added to the text.

Another area which the Enemy is exploiting relates to error and deceptive distractions which divide members of the Father's family and weaken the witness of the Christian community as a whole. Two extensive chapters on the principles and problems of discernment and deliverance have been included to meet this rather urgent need. The concept of the cross as realized in our daily lives is emphasized as a necessary part of the Christian's armor.

Every chapter has been expanded with additional insights and illustrations which have developed during the intervening years. Each has been designed to help the newly Spirit-baptized believer to become soundly grounded in God's principles and purposes for His people. Both heavenly privileges and earthly problems of the Spirit-filled life are discussed in a practical and personal way.

It is the desire of the author that the message contained in the following pages will reach the heart of the reader in a most life-refreshing way. It is with great expectation and glorious hope that together we claim the full will and purpose of our Heavenly Father for these exciting and important days just before us.

May we ever be filled-to-overflowing Christians with the life-giving Spirit of our wonderful Lord. This is our destiny, for Jesus promised that if we continued to believe in Him as the Scriptures have said, out of our innermost beings would continually flow spiritual rivers of living water (John 7:37-39).

PREFACE TO THE SECOND EDITION

The chapters on "Prayer in the Spirit," "The Spirit and God's Word," "The Spirit and Our Witness," and "The Spirit of Joy, Peace, and Love" have all been significantly expanded with additional insights and examples. One area of concern and often confusion for the Spirit-filled Christian is that of trials, testing, and temptation. Two chapters have been added in this edition to help provide the answers from God's Word: "Trials, Testing, and Temptation" and "The Temptations of the Spirit-Filled Christ." Many illustrations are drawn from the pages of both Bible history and modern-day life. May the reader of this new edition be as blessed by God's Spirit as was the author during its preparation.

1

Prayer in the Spirit

After you are filled with the Holy Spirit, you will find a whole new dimension opening up in your Christian life. Your initial experience is but the *beginning* of an exciting and wonderful adventure in the Lord. You have launched out into the "life abundant." As you mature in your experience, you need never lose its freshness. *The Holy Spirit is the never-failing Spirit of hope and expectation.*

This does not mean that there will not be trials and even persecution. In fact, the power of Satan will be felt as never before. But, you have a heavenly source in the Holy Spirit who by faith will release the power, wisdom, and love of Christ through your life each day.

Therefore, begin each day by giving the day back to God and fully committing yourself to the Holy Spirit who desires to equip, teach, and use you for His glory. Expect something new from God each day *for* you; that *through* you, He may draw others to Himself.

Faith is characterized by its object. The object of our faith is a great God. *Great faith will have great ex-*

pectations! Begin to believe for God's daily working in your life in ways that will be as wonderful and amazing as He is. "Eye hath not seen, nor ear heard, neither have entered into the heart of man, the things which God hath prepared for them that love him. But God hath revealed them unto us by His spirit" (I Cor. 2:9-10). "The things" referred to in the above passage are the "all things" which pertain to Jesus which the Holy Spirit will show unto us (John 16:15). In other words Jesus is going to become progressively more real to you than He has ever been before. You will know more and more of *His* love and *His* power and of *His* wisdom in your life! This is what it means to live a Spirit-filled life. "If we live in the Spirit, let us also walk in the Spirit" (Gal. 5:25). The spiritual walk of the Christian has direction. We are going somewhere. The "somewhere" is really to "someone" . . . Jesus Christ!

Let us see how the Holy Spirit desires to bring life to Christian experience in the areas of prayer, Bible study, and witness. We will begin with prayer.

A pastor once exclaimed right after receiving the fullness of God's Spirit in praise, "Why, prayer won't be a chore anymore!" He was absolutely right. The Holy Spirit is the Spirit of prayer. When we by faith close ourself off to pray "with God's Spirit," we are entering into a most meaningful experience. There is indeed a refreshing and a release. *Prayer should be as alive as is the God to whom we pray.* One of the most deadening things in Christian experience is "saying -rayers," instead of talking to God.

I can remember during "circle prayers" awaiting my turn and carefully rehearsing what and how I was going to pray. Occasionally, someone else would "steal" my prayer before my turn came, and I would be left high and dry and at a loss for words. I somehow

2

suspect that my part of the prayer circle was about as unsatisfactory to God as it was empty for me. I have since discovered that I was not alone in such frustrations, although this is really of little comfort. How hollow our prayers can sometimes be! It is the desire of the Holy Spirit to fill our lives with praise and prayer. He neither slumbers nor sleeps and prays without ceasing. *If we are filled with God's Spirit, we are filled with never-failing prayer!*

By faith we can "tune in" to the Spirit of prayer and "with Him" lift heavenward our confessions, intercessions, petitions, and praise. No wonder Paul encourages us to pray "with our spirit as moved by His Spirit" (I Cor. 14:15 Wuest). This truth is further reinforced in Ephesians 6:18 and Jude 20 where we are admonished to pray "in, by means of, through" the Holy Spirit that we might stand strong and be built up in the most holy faith (various translations).

Praying in tongues and with our understanding is an active expression of *a living faith in a living God.* One of the most exciting experiences of the Spirit-filled life is that God really does answer prayer. To *say* it is one thing; to *see* it is another. If we say it in faith, we will see it in life . . our life!

A professional colleague of mine has just recently been filled with the Holy Spirit. A brush fire was threatening the home of a mutual friend early one Sunday afternoon. An appeal for prayer was made, and we all responded by seeking God's protection for their home. The flames were checked and their home was saved. My colleague later told us of their prayer experience at the time. They had taken time out from the activities of Sunday dinner and had prayed an earnest but short prayer for God's intervention. He immediately felt that God had heard and would act accordingly. They rejoiced but were not surprised to

3

learn of the outcome. "It's a funny thing," he said, "but before being filled with God's Spirit, I never would have had that kind of faith." Jesus is the Author and Finisher of our faith (Heb. 12:2). *The Holy Spirit of faith simply makes Him more real to us!*

OUR PRAYER OF PRAISE

There are several different expressions to prayer. We have already mentioned the purpose and power in praise. *Praise is a very positive expression of our faith!* It should be a continual part of our daily experience. Our last thoughts at night and our first thoughts in the morning should be those of praise to God. As a compass needle immediately swings to the north when distracting forces are removed, so should our minds go fleeting back to God in worship all through the day as we move from one mental task to another. A great deal of God's power can quickly be compressed into our lives as periodically we lift our voices, audibly or inaudibly as the occasion may allow, to Him in divinely directed praise. There is great edifying power in praying in tongues all throughout the day. Here is one way we can repeatedly "tune in" to the unceasing Spirit of praise who faithfully fills our lives with His presence.

Someone once raised the question, "Do you claim to be able to pray in tongues anytime you want to? Isn't that like turning God on and off according to your whim and fancy?" I had never thought of the abiding privilege of Spirit-inspired prayer quite in that sense before, and I had no desire to be turning Him "on and off" like a water faucet. I asked the Lord about this. His reply was simple and direct as is so often the case. "Don't worry about it," He responded; "I am always on! . . . You are the one who needs to be turned on in faith. My unceasing Spirit of prayer will ever be ready to respond." I have never worried about the question since. God is always faithful, and He is always worthy of our praise.

Some time ago we received a letter from a lady and her husband whom it had been our privilege to lead into the fullness of the Holy Spirit. She was describing the new joy that God had brought to their lives and how Thanksgiving Day had been the most wonderful Thanksgiving they had ever spent together.

Then she shared something I will never forget. "Do you notice," she said, "that we seem to be saying 'Praise God' more since we 'received'? The words 'Praise God' flow so easily from our lips, and these words seem to be definitely connected with our heart. Anyway, I seem to get a little 'pang' when I say it."

This really touched my heart. In fact, it brings tears to my eyes just to think about it again. I know what she was talking about! The Holy Spirit has a way of linking our hearts with Jesus when we praise Him that brings a thrill to this earthly life of ours. To know the touch of Jesus is to be spoiled for anything else as far as *real* joy in this world is concerned. How, apart from His Spirit, could we ever praise Him as we should?

Wonder and worship are very closely related. We live in a truly wonderful world. In spite of the disorder, pain, and violence which have scarred the face of nature as a result of man's original sin, the fingerprints of a loving Creator are to be seen on every hand if one is looking for that touch of God. From the delicate design and sparkling symmetry of a snowflake to the magnificent expanse of the starry heavens, the wonders of God's handiwork are displayed for those who wish to see. Our natural world becomes a window through which the glory of God floods in upon our lives. *Our response in praise lifts our earthly sense of wonder into the heavenly dimension of worship!*

I remember when the Lord impressed me that in one sense the entire universe waits upon us for the fulfillment of its purpose in creation. The one hundred forty-eighth Psalm speaks of the sun, moon, and stars of light; the fire, hail, snow, and stormy winds; the mountains, hills, fruitful trees, and all cedars; the beasts, cattle, creeping things, and flying fowl as all praising God. (This covers the entire range of mineral, plant, and animal kingdoms.) Isaiah, the poetic prophet, refers to the mountains and the hills as breaking forth into singing and the trees of the field and forest as clapping their hands for peace and joy (Isa. 44:23; 55:12).

For praise, love, or worship to be truly satisfying to God, however, it must be freely and meaningfully expressed. True appreciation and affection involves a level of awareness and willingness which only human personality possesses. Only man was endowed with the sovereignty and rational and emotional capacity to love the Lord with all his heart, soul, and mind and to consciously live to the praise of His glory! (Matt. 22:37; Eph. 1:12).

"The heavens declare the glory of God," but only to the listening ear of someone who can perceive that wonder and translate it into heartfelt praise. The sweet song of the meadowlark in the early morning waits for us to lift its note of joy and freedom heavenward upon the wings of our worship. There is no other way! All of creation waits—as does the Lord Himself —upon our response to the wonder of our Father's world. I am amazed — just amazed — to think that God has given to us that wonderful privilege of personally completing both the pleasure and purpose for

6

which He created the heavens and the earth and all that is therein!

> Thou art worthy, O Lord, to receive glory and honor and power: for thou hast created all things, and for thy pleasure they are and were created .... Praise waiteth for Thee, O God! (Rev. 4:11; Ps. 65:1).

As wonder is but a step away from worship, so praise is a comely partner for God-given pleasures. There was a time when I thought anything in which I found pleasure was automatically evil. What a warped concept of our Heavenly Father the Enemy (and sometimes people) puts into our hearts. I recall thoroughly enjoying a symphony concert some years ago and suddenly being stricken with the thought that I was finding far too much pleasure in something that wasn't a "sacred" hymn! How very ready the Holy Spirit was to sanctify the moment with my praise, but It had given way to a false sense of guilt, and both the Lord and I were the losers!

It is true we can become so possessed by our desire for earthly pleasures that we lose the heavenly joy of following Jesus, but this is not necessary. God would have us possess our pleasures for His glory and praise. *We are to praise Him in all things — this includes our pleasures as well as our pain!*

Paul had discovered the strength and stability that the Spirit of joy and praise can bring to both the pain and pleasures of life. He had learned to rejoice in all things and at all times — regardless! He knew how to face both prosperity and poverty without losing his spiritual balance (Phil. 4:11-13). Praise is like the balancing pole used by professional wire-walkers in the circus. It keeps them from falling to the right or to the left.

Praising God in tongues can become a sensitive thermometer for the Spirit-filled Christian. Only a life filled with God will continually want to praise Him. Conversely, one of the first dimensions to go in a life where the Holy Spirit has been grieved will be the desire to praise God. The Spirit of worship has been quenched. Our communion with the Holy Spirit around the praiseworthiness of God's Son has been broken. *Even the slightest sin unconfessed will dampen our desire to praise the Lord!*

I have found in my own life that this is one of the ways the Holy Spirit will most quickly and specifically bring to my attention some sin that needs to be confessed. It is impossible to praise God in tongues and be irritated at one's children at the same time. God has a way of desiring our praise in the midst of most "earthy" situations. *Any attitude of heart or mind which robs God of the praise He deserves is sin.* As soon as it is confessed in faith, our communion with the Holy Spirit in Christ is restored. So is our joy and peace in the Lord. In this way, the purifying power of praise can find a very practical function in our daily lives.

We can learn all kinds of lessons from everyday situations. Once I asked the Lord to help me find a parking place when conditions were crowded and I was in a hurry. What a delight it was to see someone suddenly pull out just in time to allow me to pull in. How easy and right it was to praise the Lord.

However, on another occasion when I was anxious to be on time for an appointment, the same prayer seemed powerless. In fact, after circling endlessly, I finally waited for someone I saw about to enter his car and make his exit. He did, but someone who had just come into the lot, moving in the wrong direction, neatly maneuvered into my anticipated slot. I had almost been tempted to race my way to the parking place, but knew I couldn't make it anyway. The thought, however, had already discharged my sympathetic nervous system, and adrenalin was now circulating in high concentration. The tight, tense, sick-inside feeling, coupled with the flush of anger and the cold-sweat of resentment (the calling-fire-from-heaven-on-their-heads syndrome) pretty well possessed me for the moment. Now what does one do? Praise God! Praise God — for what?? Praise God for the fruit of patience and long-suffering! This is the only kind of ground in which it can grow. Not only that, *praise is the best tranquilizer in the whole world.* It takes power to praise God in the midst of adversity. Many situations are far more serious than a crowded parking lot, but the indwelling, ready-to-flow Spirit of praise can provide the power we need in our weakness. It is a sweet victory to experience. (The principle of power through praise is developed in depth in Merlin Carothers' book, *Prison to Praise,* Logos, International, Plainfield, N.J.)

Praise also is often the fountainhead from which other manifestations of the Spirit stream forth. At the close of a morning worship service where I had spoken, an elderly lady approached me for prayer. Symptoms of a former illness involving cancer were returning, and she requested the ministry of healing. I felt no great surge of faith and was a little reluctant to pray before confessing the faithful presence of the Lord. I suggested we worship God together and allow Him to inhabit our praises with His life-giving power. As we began to pray in the Spirit, God moved upon her with such force I was afraid she was going to fall over. Our faith reached forth for her healing, and I immediately ministered to her with the laying on of hands. Her symptoms disappeared like shadows flee from the

9

light and warmth of the early morning sun. How faithfully the Son of righteousness arises with healing in His wings when beckoned by the praises of God's people (Mal. 4:2).

Her daughter then came forward and confessed her need for deliverance from the bondage of fear and depression. As we prayed, I encouraged her to respond to the Spirit in worship, and she immediately broke forth in a heavenly tongue, glorifying and magnifying God. Needless to say, the Lord exchanged her spirit of heaviness for the garment of praise! (Isa. 61:3).

One final illustration came to my attention shortly after the first edition of this book was published. One of my students joyfully told me of an older friend who was in the hospital with a painful spinal problem. As he was reading alone in his room, the simplicity of worshiping God by His Spirit in faith, regardless of circumstances, reached his heart. With great gladness he lifted his voice in spontaneous praise, completely lost in the holy wonder of God's glorious presence. At that moment the oil of joy became God's healing balm as well, and he was instantly delivered from his infirmity and subsequently discharged from the hospital. What a beautiful confirmation of God's Word that He does indeed inhabit the praises of His people! (Ps. 22:3).

OUR PRAYER OF CONFESSION

We now rather naturally come to another expression of prayer, that of confession. *Confession in prayer must always be of a twofold nature, negative and positive.* "Negatively" we confess our sins, mistakes, failures, imperfections, and great need. We readily confess all that we are not. And, in ourselves, we are nothing! Then in faith and with rejoicing, we "positively" confess our Savior, His forgiveness, His perfection, and our righteousness in Him. We readily confess all that He is. And, in Him, we have everything!

Satan is very subtle and will always try to limit our confession to repeated negatives. Sometimes he will point an accusing finger at some defect in our life and through continual condemnation drive us to despair and discouragement. Our testimony at such a time is completely neutralized, and God's will for our lives frustrated. This is one way Satan endeavors to undermine our witness for Christ. *We should be prepared to overcome such an evil spirit of despair by actively presenting a positive confession of our faith.*

An occasion in our own lives required just such an expression of our faith before the darkness of discouragement was defeated. I had been invited to speak at a Christian Advance meeting in Riverside, California. The weather was hot, and by late afternoon our entire family was tired and a little on the edgy side. To make matters worse, we lost our way, and I was growing fearful that we might be late. As time progressed, I became more irritable within and sharp-spoken without. Before long, however, the Holy Spirit faithfully impressed me with how grievous this was to the Lord. I had no sooner confessed my failure than this barbed thought flashed through my mind: *How can I stand before an audience tonight and minister the peace and joy of the Lord when my own life has been such an obvious contradiction?* My heart sank in despair, and a fear bordering on inner panic overwhelmed me. God's faithful Spirit then brought a word of hope to my remembrance. Had God not said that "if we confess our sins, he is faithful and just to forgive us our sins, and to cleanse us from all unrighteousness"? (I John 1:9). This meant simply that we would again be clean and

11

fit vessels for God's Spirit to fill. God said so! I immediately made this positive confession with my full understanding quickened by the Holy Spirit. As a further expression of faith, I moved on into devotional tongues allowing this release to be a means of "washing from my life" the inner tensions and confusion. As the Holy Spirit used this means of grace to edify my life, an awareness of His peace brought a quietness to my troubled soul.

That night, God's hand of evident blessing was upon His Word, and in a most encouraging way, God confirmed to me again the overcoming power which He brings to a positive confession of faith. *The Holy Spirit will always honor a positive confession of God's Word!* If we confess anything less than this, the Spirit is grieved, and we quench His work and witness in our lives. This is the reason some prayers seem so gray and lifeless.

A Catholic lady once confided in me that God always seemed so far away and that it was necessary for her to work her way into His presence through the effort of prayer. One day after being baptized in the Holy Spirit by Jesus, she was in her church praying. Subconsciously she was again endeavoring to break her way through into the heavenlies. Suddenly the whole church seemed to be flooded with the glowing warmth of God's presence. She then heard these words within her heart: *"Do not pray as if I am far off and not easily entreated, for I have come to dwell within your heart, where we may enjoy constant communion with each other."* She said a warmth flooded her innermost being, and to this day the intimate awareness of her Lord's presence has brought a simple beauty to her prayer and devotions she had never known before. How very much God longs to have our love and fellowship!

The Holy Spirit also desires that we confess the ever-abiding presence of Jesus within our lives. Since the fullness of the Godhead dwelleth in Him (Col. 2:9), there is something of the mystery of the Trinity which resides in our lives and in our fellowship with each other here on the earth. There is an intimate relationship with the Father Himself which we enjoy through Jesus. Here indeed is a mystery, but it satisfies the desire of the Father to be with His children. Yes, in one sense, the Son, as to His Person, is at the right hand of the Father in heaven. Yet in another way, through the communion of the Holy Spirit, their presence is as close to us as the very air we breathe!

OUR PRAYER OF INTERCESSION

Another dimension in our prayer is related to intercession. Here, by faith, we allow the Holy Spirit to *identify* ourselves with a personal need, and at the same time to *identify* ourselves with the divine supply which is in the Lord Jesus. The intercessory prayer of faith bridges heaven and earth on behalf of someone that God has laid upon our hearts. *We become God's link of love.* Jesus was and is an intercessor. If we are to become like Him, we, too, will allow the Spirit of intercession to move us in prayer.

Praying in tongues gives intercessory prayer a powerful dimension. Perhaps at no other time do we more keenly feel the limitations of our understanding. The force of our prayer is weakened by the fact that we do not know how to pray as we ought. How good of God to provide a way which bypasses the limitations of our minds and of our speech! We know that divinely expressed intercession will always be in keeping with God's divine purposes. This provides a real safeguard for our prayers and allows our faith to find full

13

expression without reservations concerning His will.

How easy it is for us sometimes to program somebody else's life! We begin to project into our prayer what we think would be God's will for their situation. Just recently we have seen the Lord answer our prayers for someone in a most unusual way. It was something we never would have anticipated. God very clearly showed us the danger of limiting Him by tending to rely upon our understanding alone. God works in ways which to man are mysterious. *Praying in tongues is one way that the mysteries of God can be spoken without passing through the restricting filter of our minds.*

A wife and mother in her early fifties approached me at the end of a Bible class and requested that we pray for her inner needs concerning a serious personal problem in her family. We had prayed with her some months earlier and God had brought an inner healing to her life, and there were evidences of a healing work in her home as well.

Recent reverses, coupled with physical distress, had painfully pressed her to a place of lonely desperation which prompted her plea for help from me and some of her sisters in the Lord who had remained behind after the class had concluded. Not sensing the seriousness nor the intensity of her inner anguish, I encouraged her to keep praising the Lord, with a little feeling of impatience concerning her lack of faith. How cruel and void of compassion we sometimes can be with others, even while endeavoring to minister God's Word! I have discovered *the truth can kill as quickly as error if it is not ministered in love and with Christian grace!*

The Holy Spirit sharply reproved my soul within, and I realized God wanted us to intercede on behalf of our sister without further discussion. (There are times

14

when prayer is preferable to words.) We gathered around her and began to pray with both faith and feeling for her personal need. As we were thus holding her up in prayer, she suddenly collapsed to the floor . . . into the arms of Jesus! As we knelt by her prostrate form, I realized she had reached her emotional, physical, and spiritual limits, so pressed was she in soul. *Fortunately, our limits are not God's!*

We continued to intercede for her and encouraged her to allow the Holy Spirit to intercede on her behalf. She began praying in her heavenly tongue with spiritual groanings that could not otherwise have been expressed. *There are times when only the Holy Spirit Himself can completely encompass the inner anguish of our souls.* She had come for spiritual ministry, and the faithful intercession of the Holy Spirit prevailed.

A powerful surge of spiritual authority rose up within us, and we challenged Satan to his face in the almighty name of Jesus! We rebuked the spirit of depression and released our sister into the joy and peace of her Lord. Her whole expression changed, and she triumphantly arose as a true daughter of the King! It was like watching Lazarus come forth from the tomb! The resurrection power of Him who ever liveth to make intercession for us had prevailed again (Heb. 7:25). We all joined together in praise and thanksgiving for God's abundant grace and mercy for our sister (Isa. 59:16).

Another very beautiful illustration was shared with me recently by the wife of a Swedish brother in the Lord who had rather suddenly been taken to his heavenly home. He had always felt a burden for his family in Sweden, yearning that they, too, might come to know the joy he had found in the Lord Jesus. Although he was a careful and successful business-man, his relationship with the Lord was simple and

15

sincere and his faith childlike — the kind that leads one into the wonders of God's Kingdom. On occasion, the Spirit of the Lord would grace his life with a heavenly vision or dream.

One such experience involved a conversation with the Lord Jesus in which he shared with great feeling his concern and deep desire that his loved ones might find God in the same heartfelt way that was so real to him. The Lord listened with great understanding and then responded, "Oscar, why don't you and I join together and pray for them right now!" With that, Jesus took his hand, and they united their voices in intercessory prayer. To his amazement, he found he was clothed in a beautiful bright garment. In the morning he was led by the Holy Spirit to an understanding concerning the significance of this unusual scene through the references to white robes found in the Book of Revelation:

> Yet even there in Sardis some haven't soiled their garments with the world's filth; they shall walk with me in white, for they are worthy. Everyone who conquers [overcomes] will be clothed in white. . . . (Rev. 3:4-5 TLB)

Could we find a promise here for those who choose to overcome through prayer, that theirs shall be a walk in white with Jesus — a special hand-in-hand ministry of intercession which shall prevail? Shortly thereafter, Oscar had the great joy while visiting in Sweden to lead his own brother to Christ just before his brother died. Oscar's own death sometime thereafter was the occasion for a very moving witness to other members of his family. And now his memory is still faithfully pointing others to Jesus. One wonders if his earthly ministry of intercession with

16

Jesus is continuing still on the heavenly side! Certainly our great High Priest, the Lord Jesus Himself, ever liveth to make intercession for us (Heb. 7:25; 4:14-16). *There is perhaps no more beautiful or needed ministry than that of intercessory prayer!* (Isa. 59:16).

OUR PRAYERS OF PETITION

Lastly, let us consider our prayers of petition. Jesus said that if we would ask anything in His name, He would do it that the Father would be glorified in the Son (John 14:13). The "anything" is qualified in a twofold way. First of all, *we must present the name of Jesus with our petition.* That name represents who He is and what He has accomplished for us.

The name also represents who we are in Him! When we were born into God's family through the life of Jesus as our Savior, we not only inherited His nature but also received His name. We have been baptized into His body and are accepted in the Beloved and thereby bear His name for God's glory. There is legal authority in the name of Jesus and the power of the Holy Spirit to execute that authority. As we move in faith, our prayers should become as strong as those that Jesus prayed! "As my Father hath sent me, even so send I you" (John 20:21).

Secondly, *what we ask for must be so related to Jesus that it will bring glory to the Father.* In other words, everything in our lives, whether large or small, earthly or heavenly, people, places, or things, is to revolve around God's Son. Every prayer must place Jesus in its center! If we are sure of this, then we can ask anything in all confidence.

Sometimes God honors our prayer of faith by giving us the desires of our hearts rather than the petitions we have requested. God-given desires can occasionally be misdirected when it comes to the way in which we may anticipate their fulfillment. Praying in the Spirit that our understanding may be clear concerning the timing and fashion of God's answer is important. Our natural minds have a peculiar way of fastening onto an immediate answer which has personal appeal. Our prayers then follow in line unless we recognize the little red flags the Holy Spirit raises as warning signals.

A student of mine was having great difficulty in mastering the prescribed courses for his premedical major. We had talked and prayed together with little result as far as the academic area of his life was concerned. After several semesters, it was obvious that medicine was most definitely not his calling. Yet he seemed reluctant to consider any other alternatives for his life. As we shared further together, the following picture finally emerged:

He and one of his close friends had a strong and sincere desire to serve God and be used of Him in ministering to others. They agreed together in prayer to make the medical profession the direction for their lives. The young man's parents were proud and pleased, and subsequently allowed no other alternative to be raised for possible consideration. The two students often prayed together, but only the other boy satisfactorily completed his course and subsequently was accepted into medical school.

It was apparent that God was trying to speak, but a preconceived set of mind precluded the possibility of a hearing until the circumstances forced a confrontation with reality. As we talked together, we recognized that the boy's desire to share the love of God with people was put into his heart by the Lord. He excelled in sports and worked with underprivileged youngsters at the local Y.M.C.A. He also enjoyed history but had never seriously considered teaching in either of these areas because his goal had already been rigidly set.

God broke a heavy yoke that day as a young man made the glorious discovery that the Lord could answer the desire of his prayers in a way somewhat different than he had petitioned! He opened himself in faith and expectation to a whole new direction in life for Christian service. A teaching major in history with a minor in physical education fitted his personality and God's will for his life like green fits the color of grass.

Did God answer his prayer? Yes, in a far more wonderful way for him than he previously had ever thought possible. Maybe we all should examine our petitions more carefully before we try to force an answer where it was never intended to fit. What freedom and faith our prayers can have when we finally allow God Himself to shape the answer for the need!

Finally, our prayers of petition should never become commonplace. We may pray in common places but always with an awareness that God is near and hears every word. Some time ago my wife attended a small prayer-and-share group in Tulsa, Oklahoma. Following the prayer time, one of the ladies approached my wife and said, "As you were praying, I saw Jesus standing beside you with His hand upon your head." When she shared this with me, I couldn't help but think that God in His grace sometimes pushes back the curtains of this earthly life of ours just enough for us to see how very close He really is. Many of the prayers offered that night have already been answered. God really does answer prayer!

THE PREVAILING POWER
OF PERSISTENT PRAYER

The Adversary will ever seek to place a seal upon

our lips when it comes to our prayer and praise. He is well aware of the power which is released when by faith we strike through to this mighty stream of God's Spirit. Subtle and devious are Satan's ways, and we need to recognize the methods which he employs.

In the early days of our life in the Spirit, the Lord taught me an unforgettable lesson. A group of college students who had recently been Spirit-baptized were meeting weekly in our home. On one such evening I was awaiting their arrival in a spirit of expectant prayer and praise. How thankful we were for all that God had so sovereignly been doing in our midst! Soon the time for their arrival came, but no one made an appearance. My praise began to dwindle and finally faded out altogether. Time moved on and the silent doorbell became an object of irritation and resentment. Dark thoughts flooded my mind concerning the unkind and unfair remarks some people had made concerning the character and conduct of our fellowship. *Why didn't they come and see for themselves, or talk firsthand with some of the students whose lives had been so graciously changed?* I wondered.

It seemed that some cruel, restraining influence had discouraged the meeting as planned. I was deeply and personally distressed at heart. At this point the Holy Spirit reminded me that a few days earlier He had revealed to me that God's children could face any situation with the faith, hope, and love of Jesus. As if in contrast, my mind had been darkened by doubt, despair, and resentment. At first, I was a little annoyed to have my thought pattern so abruptly broken, even if it was by the voice of the Lord! However, I quickly confessed my sinful attitude and accepted God's forgiveness. He then prompted me to praise Him regardless of the circumstances. I responded by praying forth in tongues, although the effort was admittedly somewhat less than vigorous.

Immediately I was challenged by the Devil. I was informed that my praise was both hollow and hypocritical. I was not praying from my heart at all, but merely mouthing syllables which were both mechanical and meaningless. The accusation so accurately matched my feelings that the only honest and reasonable thing to do was to stop praying at once. And, I did!

I am both amazed and thankful for the patient but persistent ministry of the Holy Spirit in His discipline of our lives. I had no sooner stopped praying than God began to deal with me in a stern but very positive way. The sequence of thoughts was somewhat as follows:

"My son, haven't I taught you certain principles from My Holy Word?"

"Yes, Lord," I replied.

"And haven't I instructed you plainly that praying in tongues is not primarily a matter of feeling but of faith; and is not the time you need to pray the most the very time you feel like it the least?"

"Yes, Lord."

"Haven't I made it clear to you that when you are praying in the Spirit, you are permitting a heavenly expression which goes beyond the reason and understanding of your natural mind?"

"Yes, Lord."

"Haven't I specifically indicated to you that My Spirit will faithfully intercede for you when you don't even know how to pray as you ought?"

"Yes, Lord."

"And finally, didn't I warn you against measuring everything in terms of your blessing? Is not your prayer of faith well pleasing and a blessing to Me?"

"Yes, Lord."

"Then, My son, you must make up your mind. Are you going to put your faith and confidence in Me, My Word, My Son, and My Spirit, or in how you think and feel under the circumstances?"

I immediately told the Lord I was sorry; He was right and I had been wrong again. I asked for His forgiveness, and proceeded to forcefully pray in the Spirit without hesitation and without ceasing. There was no sense of overwhelming joy or happiness, only a sure sense of rightness. I continued for some time to pray as God had instructed me to do.

Then it happened! There was a knock on the door and the late arrivals suddenly made their appearance. Needless to say, at that moment I experienced a great deal of feeling and the meeting that followed was a most joyful occasion. Afterward, the Lord impressed me again concerning the power of prayer and praise. *Every answer begins in heaven in the realm of the Spirit before it is seen on earth in the realm of the natural!*

Sometimes the answer is not immediately forthcoming as in the example above, for such experiences are placed in our lives as lessons. *The man of faith, however, will persist in prayer and praise regardless of what the eye sees, the mind thinks, or the heart feels!*

In regard to feelings, I was further instructed of the Lord by a rather unusual thought. It was as if God wanted me to understand how easy it is for the Adversary to deceive us if we are not aware of his ways. He will even quote Scripture for his own purposes. (It is usually out of context and always misinterpreted and misdirected.) In the example above, the Scripture passage which Satan used to condemn me is found in Mark 7:6:

Well hath Esaias prophesied of you hypocrites, as

it is written, This people honoureth me with their lips, but their heart is far from me.

The context had to do with a people who had willfully hardened their hearts against God. This was not the way it was applied to my situation at all. To clarify the matter for me, the Spirit of God raised this question for me: "My son, what is in your heart?" I thought for a moment and then replied, "Well, Your Son, Your Spirit, Your Word are all in my heart." It was as if God then responded, "What do you mean then by suggesting your prayer was not from your heart? Is not My Holy Spirit the unceasing Spirit of praise and worship? Is not My Son the fountainhead for My Spirit and the author of your faith? Is He not the object of your affection and praise? Are you not basing your privilege and responsibility for prayer and worship upon the authority of My Word? Am I not ever-faithful on your behalf and always worthy of your worship? Am I not willing and ready to receive your prayer if you offer it to me in faith and obedience? *But of course your prayer was from your heart — that is the reason the devil tried to put a seal on your lips; he knows very well the power in prayer and praise!*"

These impressions from the Lord concluded with this obvious but powerful revelation: "What Satan really means when he says your prayer is not from your heart, is that it is not primarily sourced in your natural feelings. And, My son, your feelings are the most unstable part of your life! Nowhere in My Word have I ever indicated that the only time you may pray or worship is when you feel like it. I am both faithful and worthy — regardless of how you feel or think. Confess that in faith, and you shall have the confirming witness (inner knowing) of My Spirit!"

What added meaning we now find in the familiar

promise of our Lord, "For everyone who keeps on asking, receives; and the one who keeps on seeking, finds; and to the one who keeps on knocking, the door will open" (Luke 11:10 Williams). We, too, with Jesus, can simply but confidently confess, "Father, I thank You that You have heard Me. Yes, I know You always hear and listen to Me" (John 11:41-42 TAB).

PRAYER THROUGH SPIRITUAL SONG

The apostle Paul indicates it is the privilege of Spirit-filled believers to sing both in the understanding — our earthly tongue — and in the Spirit — our heavenly tongue (I Cor. 14:15). This is a beautiful expression of praise and worship in which both the melody and associated syllables are prompted by the Holy Spirit. Such a spiritual song has a soft, sweet beauty which is clear and pure in its quality. Many find this release during their initial experience in Holy Spirit Baptism.

Undoubtedly this same lovely expression of worship is referred to in Paul's letter to the Ephesians (5:18-19):

Be ever filled with the Holy Spirit; your tongues unloosed in psalms, hymns, and spiritual songs, singing and making melody in your hearts to the Lord! (various translations)

As with praying in the Spirit, singing in the Spirit can be expressed privately in one's own personal devotion or in unison with others in a believers' meeting. It is one means of magnifying the Lord together in the harmony of the Spirit. *The Amplified Bible* translates a portion of the above passage as follows: "Speak out to one another in . . . spiritual songs, offering praise with

24

voices." This may have been a part of the unison praise which characterized the Pentecostal experience at the house of Cornelius: "For they heard them speak with [other] tongues and magnify God" (Acts 10:46).

Often after a time of singing together in the understanding, the Holy Spirit will move a group of Spirit-filled believers into a sustained song in which both voices and melody are harmoniously blended into a beautiful anthem of praise. There is a soft, restful beauty to such worship that always reminds me of the soothing effect of warm fragrant, anointing oil.

I have discovered in my private devotions that praying in the Holy Spirit often very naturally leads into singing in the Spirit. This may initially involve a deliberate exercise in faith. Paul indicates the role of the *will* that is involved. "I *will* pray . . . (and) sing in the Spirit." As an expression of love and adoration, we lift our voices in any little tune that we feel like expressing. (The Holy Spirit of worship immediately cooperates with our efforts.) Sometimes we simply begin by humming softly to the Lord from our hearts filled with praise. As we add Spirit prompted syllables, our heavenly tune becomes a spiritual song!

Many may have come close to such worship without realizing what was happening. I was talking with a monk one day in a Trappist Monastery near Ogden, Utah. He was asking me questions about praying and singing in the Spirit. We explained to him the meaning and significance of this lovely privilege for all Spirit-filled believers as discussed in some detail in our book, *Aglow with the Spirit*.

He looked at me with great amazement and exclaimed, "Why, I have been doing that for a long time and didn't know what it was." I asked him to share his experience with me. "Well," he said, "I used to cut wood alone back up in the hills for the monastery.

While there in my solitude, I would spontaneously sing and praise the Lord from a heart overflowing with love. After a time, I discovered I couldn't put into words how I really felt about the Lord, and so I decided I would just make up a language with which I could praise and sing without inhibition!" As you probably have already surmised, God had seen the desire of his heart, and although he was not aware of the scriptural basis for the experience, it was definitely of the Holy Spirit. We then worshiped and magnified the name of the Lord together in sweet praise and spiritual song. How very gracious of God!

This can be your joy as well, even now, if you also wish to so yield to the Holy Spirit in praise and worship. Begin by softly sighing or humming in the Spirit. Let it come from your innermost being with great affection and love to God. As you include soft little unknown syllables, the "melody in your heart" will become a "song in the Spirit." By the time your song reaches heaven, all the heavenly host will have joined in with angelic anthems of glorious praise! (This might be closer to the truth than we imagine [Rev. 5:8-14; Pss. 148, 149, 150].)

To be filled with the Spirit is to be filled with the power of unceasing prayer and praise!

2

The Spirit and God's Word

THE LOGOS OF LIFE

In the beginning was the Word and the Word was with God, and the Word was God. . . . And the Word was made flesh, and dwelt among us, (and we beheld His glory, the glory as of the only begotten of the Father,) full of grace and truth. (John 1:1, 14)

The Greek word for "Word" in the New Testament passage above is "logos." It is a term which in its richest philosophical sense refers to a comprehension of concept, the totality of thought or an ideational reality which is fully expressed. *Jesus Christ is thus presented as the Divine Intention personified — the mind and heart of God realized in human form!*

He is the unique, personal, and living expression of God's love and wisdom in a manner which man can apprehend. In other words, Jesus is the "big idea" of what our Heavenly Father is really like in terms that we can understand, and to which we can warmly and personally relate.

The Holy Spirit Himself confirms the concept expressed above in the following passage from Scripture:

> Whereas in many parts and in many ways of old, God spoke to our forefathers in the words of the prophets, in this final age He has spoken to us in the person of His Son . . . Who is the outshining of His glory and the exact image and flawless expression of His very nature.
>
> For in Christ God gives a full and complete expression of Himself in human form. (Heb. 1:1-3, Col. 2:9 various translations)

What an exciting privilege it is to become better acquainted with God through the Lord Jesus as the Holy Spirit faithfully reveals to us the Person of the Living Word. It is the ministry of the Spirit to ever press us beyond the "letter" to the "Life" of God Himself. Very quickly we shall find that the Father's purpose in Jesus is the integrating theme throughout Holy Scripture. God's full will centers in His Son, and this truth is progressively revealed as one moves from Genesis to Revelation. We become an integral part of God's holy way when we become identified with His Spirit. *It is in God's Word that we discover the meaning of His will and way for our lives!*

One of the first things that newly Spirit-filled believers discover is that the Word of God has suddenly become alive for them in a new way. Many have been the times that we have been amazed at the fresh insights from God's Word that have been shared with us by college students who had recently come to know the fullness of the Holy Spirit in their lives. This should not be surprising, however, for as mentioned above, it is the purpose of the Holy Spirit to *illumi-*

nate our understanding of God's Word (I Cor. 2).

It is most interesting when we become aware that the books of the New Testament were written by Spirit-filled believers to Spirit-filled believers. The authors of the Epistles took for granted that the recipients of their divinely inspired letters had already received both the gifts of God's Son and His Spirit. Pentecostal experience was the rule, not the exception. A greater appreciation and understanding of the Scriptures are obtained when we realize that the grand themes of the Epistles find expression in our lives through the spiritual fruit and gifts. *The Word of God is the raw material the Holy Spirit uses to build Christ into our lives. As we live in the Word, the life of the Word becomes ours!*

INFORMED-TRANSFORMED-CONFORMED

The other morning I awoke with three words repeatedly going through my mind. They were these: informed, transformed, and conformed. As I pondered what significance the Holy Spirit would attach to this, the following thoughts began to develop. First of all, before we can become *conformed* into the image of Christ, we must willingly and faithfully expose our minds to His. The mind of God is revealed in His Word. Therefore, we must consistently expose ourselves to the Holy Scriptures. In this way we become Christ-*informed*. As we do, the Holy Spirit will *transform* and renew our minds like unto His (Rom. 12:2). We will progressively begin to think His thoughts rather than our thoughts. We will become more and more "Christ-minded." Now, our thoughts determine what we are, what we say, and what we do. Therefore, to the extent that we think as Jesus thinks, we will be, say, and do as Jesus is, says, and does. In other words, we will become *conformed* into His image! How supremely important is God's Word for your life and mine!

With these thoughts in mind, we find a freshness in these familiar passages from Holy Scripture:

For the word of God is full of life and power, and sharper than any two-edged sword, piercing to the division of soul and spirit, exposing and sifting the thoughts and purposes of the heart. . . . Indeed, all Scripture is inspired of God and is valuable for:

1. Doctrine (instruction in the faith)
2. Reproof (refuting of error, rebuking of sin)
3. Correction (divine discipline and redirection)
4. Instruction in righteousness (training of character— rightness in thought, motive, and conduct).

In this way, God's men will be well prepared at every point, fully equipped for every good work. (Heb. 4:12; II Tim. 3:16 various translations)

The application of God's Word to our lives is the fulfillment of the incarnation (the Word made flesh) through the Body of Christ. As members of that Body, we are to be living epistles, written of God and read of men (II Cor. 3:2-3). This is a rather lofty and noble truth, but its translation into life involves running through God's printing press. The latter experience has a way of flattening out our egos!

TRUTH TRANSLATED INTO LIFE

One morning years ago, I decided the time had arrived for God's justice to correct a situation which was obviously off-center. I was tired of waiting and felt confident that I was God's chosen instrument of redemption! (There was a problem, and undoubtedly the Lord wanted me to be a part of the solution — but in His way and time.) Anyway, I was carefully rehearsing what they would say, how I would respond, how they would react, etc.

I decided I would turn to God's Word and find a little encouragement, subconsciously hoping I would find something which again would confirm how right I was and how wrong they were! Picking up my Bible, I just happened to turn to the account of the betrayal in the Garden of Gethsemane. Being familiar with the story, I realized there was nothing in the text that really suited my situation. I did read along, however, but without much expectation.

Finally I came to the part that so graphically displays Peter trying to protect the Lord with his swinging sword. Here we see a self-styled champion of the faith coming upon the scene with his flying cape and flashing sword. It was a rather daring and dramatic tactic, to say the least. The results, however, were somewhat disappointing. His aim was poor (which is usually the case when our motives and means are wrong), and instead of heads rolling, only an ear was lost, and Jesus replaced even that minor trophy. Then in front of the disciples and the onlooking mob who had come for his arrest, Jesus turned to Peter and said, "Put your sword away, for all who take the sword must die by the sword!"

At this point, the Lord impressed me that I need read no further, for that was His word for me as well — *"Please put your sword away!"* The Word of God had become for me a sharp two-edged sword which had indeed cut deep into my soul, exposing the thoughts and intents of my heart. Once I saw myself and realized what I might have done, I was so thankful for His Word of warning. *Sometimes ears are not so*

31

easily replaced — or hands or feet — especially when they belong to the Body of Christ!

A WORD OF WISDOM

Sometimes when we begin to appreciate the power and authority of God's Word, we may be tempted to force that word to fit our own desires or needs rather than approach the Word of the Lord for wisdom. Both wisdom and power are in the Word of God. *Without wisdom, however, the power has no purpose, or a misdirected purpose.* We may also seek some isolated passage to support our position or even bring us comfort in our error. God has an answer for our need all right, but it may not be the answer we think.

I was very disturbed one night about a situation in Christian principle. I don't recall the details of the problem (yet it seemed so important then!), but I was deeply distressed. Furthermore, my wife had peacefully gone off to sleep, sweetly resting in the Lord. Peaceful expressions on people's faces can be very annoying when one is being eaten alive by inner irritation. I was almost tempted to poke my wife with my elbow and inform her this was no time to be peaceful when there was so much to worry about. A few passing thoughts crossed my mind about what a fine helpmate she turned out to be!

I finally decided to turn to God's Word for a little comfort in my hour of great anguish. I was sure the Lord would justify my position in the problem and encourage me to stay true to the faith — maybe even defend it! (I sometimes have to go through more than one lesson before God gets His point across.)

I began to search in the Psalms, but to my amazement, the passages which on previous occasions had meant so much to me now seemed like nothing more than mere sentimental sayings. The Proverbs, which before had often brought counsel and wisdom, took on the form of little pious platitudes. So on through the Bible I went, with every part seeming utterly flat and lifeless. I finally reached the Book of Revelation and was quite sure there was nothing in all the fire, smoke, and hard-to-understand symbols which would heal my wounded soul. (Actually, my feelings were hurt.)

I was just about to give up and turn off the light and hope I could sleep it off when I happened to glance at the first verse of chapter nineteen:

> After this I heard what sounded like a mighty shout of a great crowd in heaven, exclaiming, Hallelujah—praise the Lord! Salvation and glory (splendor and majesty) and power (dominion and authority [belong] to our God! (TAB)

It was like a shaft of light piercing through the dark night of my soul. The orientation of the entire passage was heavenward in praise rather than earthward in misery. I knew I must read on.

Again I was arrested by the same theme in verse six:

> After that I heard what sounded like the shout of a vast throng, like the boom of many pounding waves and like the roar of terrific and mighty thunderpeals, exclaiming, Hallelujah—praise the Lord! For now the Lord our God the Omnipotent —the All-Ruler—reigns! (TAB)

The little word "reigns" was lifted right out of the passage and immediately was related to the powerful description of our Christ in verse sixteen:

> And on His garment . . . and on His thigh He has

33

a name . . . inscribed, KING OF KINGS AND LORD OF LORDS! (TAB)

By now God's Word had gripped my mind and stilled my soul before Him. *We can be so noisy sometimes on the inside with all of our fears, doubts, suspicions, and anxieties rattling around that we can't even hear God's voice.* I was now ready to listen, and He spoke. The thoughts came as follows: "My son, do you believe that your Savior will rule and reign in that great day of the future as King of kings and Lord of lords?" I don't have real problems of faith when it comes to eternity, so I firmly replied, "I certainly do!" The question then moved from eternity into time. "My son, do you believe that our Christ rules and reigns right now, high here in the heavens?" I don't have difficulty or doubts about things in heaven either, so I promptly replied, "I do!" I had a feeling now of what direction the lesson was taking, and sure enough, the question moved from heaven to earth. "Can you confess the Lordship of your Christ this very moment in your life there on earth—ruling and reigning as King of kings and Lord of lords in the midst of your circumstances?"

This slowed me up a little, but I saw what it was the Lord wanted me to find from His Word. I was looking in the right place for the wrong answer! *What He wanted for me was something far greater than a little answer for a little problem—His desire for me was a fresh revelation concerning the Lordship of Jesus Christ!* I could have missed it if by His grace He had not arrested me through the power of His indwelling Holy Spirit. What a faithful companion!

Needless to say, I emphatically confessed Christ as ruling and reigning in my life, and the Holy Spirit immediately filled my heart with peace and rest. I turned off the light and joined my wife in the sweet sleep which God gives to those who trust and obey His Word.

John W. Follette, in his book *Arrows of Truth* (Gospel Publishing House), indicates the tendency we all have of approaching God's Word, trying to find the promises which we feel are the answers to our needs, and then almost commanding God to keep His Word. How much better it is to ask the Lord to first quiet our throbbing hearts and restore a right attitude within. *Then we can request that He reveal which of His promises we should confidently claim as bringing forth His will and purpose for all involved.* There is a promise for you—and God wants you to possess it in love and faith. Let us not cast away our confidence, but expectantly wait upon Him as we turn to our blessed Comforter in submission. I think it is of interest that nearly every time the Holy Spirit was referred to by Jesus as the Comforter, in the same context, He was also described as the "Spirit of truth." How closely God's Word and God's Spirit are interrelated!

SEARCHING THE SCRIPTURES

How might one practically and personally begin to "search the Scriptures daily"? First of all, it is suggested that one obtain a standard Bible with large print and wide margins. A small plastic ruler and a micropoint ball pen will provide the means for underlining pertinent passages and personalizing them with marginal notes. A good concordance, Bible dictionary, and single-volume commentary are also recommended. To this should be added a modern version of the Bible for added accuracy and freshness. Spend some time in a Bible bookstore finding the volumes which are most readable and suited to your personal preferences.

One might begin with the Gospel of John and the Book of Acts and follow the events preceding and following Pentecost. Here are the reactions of people just like you and me as they entered into this new adventure of the Spirit-filled life. Try to imagine how you would have felt and acted if you had been there. *You will soon be re-living, in your life now, much of what you read in their lives then!*

Paul's Epistle to the Colossians is a beautiful and powerful portrayal of the pre-eminence and centrality of the Lord Jesus Christ. We see Him pictured as "Lord of all." We are "complete in Him," and now the Holy Spirit wants to increasingly make Him "complete in us." This is how He becomes Lord of our life!

The full beauty and power of Christ can only be found in the Church or body of believers. In Paul's letter to the Ephesians, we see the part we are to play in the ministry of the Church. The spiritual gifts and graces are the means of equipping our lives for the edification of the Church. We will have more to say concerning this in the next section.

Even in the Old Testament, spiritual truth will find expansion when it is recast into the words, works, and person of Christ. For example, the Psalmist declares that the godly man's "delight is in the law of the Lord; and in his law doth he meditate day and night" (Ps. 1:2). The Spirit-filled Christian would recognize the added significance this has for him when he realizes that the law is God's Word and that Jesus is the living Word and fulfillment of the law. To substitute Jesus for the understanding, "The godly man's delight is in Jesus, and in Him doth he meditate day and night."

Sometimes it is meaningful to personalize spiritual *principles* and *promises* by restating the passage in the margin and inserting the pronoun "I" or "me." In this way, for instance, the spiritual principles in God's promises to Israel can become ours personally. Isaiah 43:1-2 declares: "Fear not: for I have redeemed thee, I have called thee by thy name; thou art mine. When thou passest through the waters, I will be with thee. . . ." How powerfully personal this becomes when in the margin we write, "I am not to fear. Christ has redeemed me. I have been called by name. I am His. He is with me. I shall not be overwhelmed."

CONCLUDING THOUGHTS

In conclusion, may we be reminded there is much concerning our relationship with God and each other which is exceptionally clear in Scripture. As the Spirit of God enlightens our hearts and minds, we are to follow in faith and obedience. In this way, we mature and can apprehend yet deeper truths and fathom greater mysteries. *The Lord doesn't expect us to walk in light He has not given nor to walk in the light of another.* He knows what is needful for us and when it should be received.

There are many areas of mystery in God's Word which will be revealed to His people as we follow in love and obedience. *To try to force an interpretation in rigid detail in these areas before God's time can create confusion and division!* In areas of uncertainty, we can peacefully hold the matter before the Lord. Sometimes our doubt is due to immaturity, and in time we are ready to receive and walk in greater light. At other times, our concern may be the discernment of the Lord warning us that we are approaching an area of error.

So often we want to see everything as black and

white. Either something is all right or all wrong. Often, however, we will be faced with a mixture in Christendom. Initially this presents a mottled appearance in which one must discern the truth from error. In reading different books (possibly even this one), one can be warmly blessed, and then, all of a sudden, a cold current is reached and the confirming witness is lost. This may be because error has slipped in or because a half-truth is presented as the whole truth. God has placed teachers in the Body of Christ that the Word might be rightly interpreted in a life-giving way. *A true spiritual teacher will present the truth with certainty and conviction where the Word is clear, but will approach the areas of mystery with humility and openness of heart and mind.* An overall attitude of dogmatism and a rigidity of thought which can sometimes be detected in certain ministries is good reason for caution. More will be said along these lines in a later chapter.

In traveling around our country and abroad, it has been marvelous to see how, wherever God is moving by His Spirit, a common ground of understanding is being established concerning our life together in Christ. Once again we see the unifying truth-revealing power there is in the Living Word. The written Word becomes alive with the Lord when we ask God's Spirit to break the bread afresh. It is the deep desire of the Holy Spirit to make God's Living Word our daily life. Jesus said, "I am the bread of life." May we quickly reply, "Give us our daily bread."

To be filled with the Spirit is to be filled with the purpose and power of God's Word!

3

The Spirit and Our Witness

The primary purpose of our Pentecostal experience is for power to witness to others of Jesus Christ. The word "witness" means to testify or furnish evidence of something we have seen, heard, or directly experienced. The Holy Spirit first makes Jesus Christ real to us in personal experience. He then enables us to furnish evidence of our living Lord to others by manifesting His life through us in thought, word, and deed. The fruit and gifts of the Spirit are the means by which others "see and hear" Christ in us. From this we can quickly see that the word "witness" means far more than passing out tracts or inviting someone to church, although on occasion both of these activities may be involved.

THE WITNESS OF LIFE

To live is to witness! It is not a matter of *whether* we are going to be a witness or not, but rather *what* we are going to be witnesses of and how effective that witness will be. The purpose of the Holy Spirit in our lives is that we may be a continual daily witness for Jesus Christ.

Witnessing for our Lord should be as real and natural as is our life. However, wherever, or whenever someone comes into our daily lives, he should encounter Jesus Christ. The rules for witnessing are basically very simple. *Live Christ and. love others!* The way that love is expressed may be soft and gentle, or swift and powerful. Both expressions are found in principle and practice throughout the Epistles and the Book of Acts. The Holy Spirit sometimes moves powerfully as a mighty rushing wind, and oftentimes gently as a circling dove about to alight. Such, too, was the life of Christ. In gentle love He gathered the little children around Him. In great power He evidenced His authority by setting free those who were possessed by Satan's power.

There is no greater privilege given to man than that of sharing the Gifts of God's Son and His Spirit with others. As we give ourselves and each day back to God, may we pray that He will bring someone with a prepared and open heart across our path. May we be sufficiently sensitive to God and others to recognize the encounter when it comes. And come it will, for *God will divinely order our lives to reach others if we expectantly ask Him to do so!*

Opportunities will surely come during the routine of our daily responsibilities. On other occasions we may wish to take the initiative ourselves and in a purposeful way go forth in faith and power to the "highways and hedges" beyond our usual lines of life.

Jesus urged us to pray that the Lord of the harvest would send more workers into the fields (Matt. 9:37-38). It is an honor to participate in such intercessory prayer, but even more wonderful to participate in the answer! It is as we aggressively go in faith that God will actually work with us and personally confirm His Word with the evidence of His saving and deliver-

40

ing power (Mark 16:15-20).

There are a variety of aids for witnessing which have been honored by God's Spirit in a most practical and personal way. Campus Crusade's "Four Spiritual Laws" (Arrowhead Springs, San Bernardino, California, 92403), and Billy Graham's "Do You Know the Steps to Peace with God?" (The Billy Graham Evangelistic Association, Box 779, Minneapolis, Minnesota, 55440) have been used in reaching thousands for Christ. These are little six-page leaflets that will assist an interested individual in making his personal confession of Jesus as his Savior.

The author has published a small fifty-five page booklet entitled *Life's Greatest Discovery*, which presents a witness for Christ from a scientific perspective. There are other materials available at any Bible bookstore. Ask God to help you become prepared for presenting Jesus to people in an effective and winsome way. Relate yourself to those in your Christian community who have discovered how to graciously share the Lord with others. They will be glad to encourage you to utilize the power of God's Spirit in this ministry of life.

LINKS OF LOVE

Many times we may be only one link in the chain of love which God is forging to bring some lost sheep back into the fold. There are many ways of giving a cup of cold water to another in the name of Jesus. Just to smile at someone as Jesus would smile at them is one of the simplest ways to begin witnessing. To express a genuine interest in someone as a person will often pave the way by which we can introduce them to the most wonderful Person we have ever known. What a privilege to so share the love and life of God! I believe it was Rufus Moseley who on occasion would greet a stranger with the rather disarming remark, "God loves you and He told me to tell you so!"

It is the Enemy that would stifle our witness by fear, coupled with a legalistic compulsion to duty. This is not God's Spirit of power or love and leads only to an awkward, strained situation.

I remember going to the barbership once and trying in a forced way to think of some way to witness to the barber. I was feeling more and more distressed and condemned by my silence until finally the time was gone. (In my case, haircuts are never lengthy ordeals anyway.) As I was going out the door under a dark cloud of depression, the Lord simply said, "You could have talked to him about the weather in the name of Jesus!" I realized I had shown no interest in the gentleman, in even a personal, conversational way, so preoccupied had I been with my "duty."

In a subsequent visit, the Lord brought about a rather "natural" opportunity which allowed me to share rather freely concerning the love of God for people. It began with my discovery that I had left my sweater the last time I had been in the shop. The barber then related a story about an unclaimed coat that once had been left behind.

This reminded me of a friend of ours who had picked up a hitchhiker on a cold, rainy night while on a trip. The man had no coat and was obviously in financial distress. The Lord prompted my friend to offer him one of the two coats which he had brought with him in the car. Furthermore, God told him to give the hitchhiker the better coat. He finally obeyed and willingly offered the man his coat as an expression of God's love. With that the hitchhiker broke down and wept, confessing that he had fully intended to rob my friend before the trip was over. They both rejoiced in the personal way that God had expressed His grace.

I left the barbershop with the assurance that God had blessed my witness in a rather obvious way. In addition, the Lord impressed me with the difference between a forced, legal, loveless kind of testimony and the natural, gracious, lovely way in which the power of God's Spirit can go beyond the weaknesses of our own personalities.

We should continually be alert all through each day, for God may bring opportunities our way when and where we least expect them. Many times we have found ourselves sharing God's Word in situations we could never have anticipated.

On a recent flight here on the West Coast, a rather interesting opportunity developed which illustrates some of the thoughts already expressed. I had just settled into an aisle seat with an empty seat to my side in spite of a rather crowded plane. I was somewhat weary and so was grateful for the opportunity to stretch out and relax without being crowded, as is so often the case. At that very moment, the stewardess approached me and inquired if I would mind moving to another seat so a father and his little boy could sit together. She then relocated me between two gentlemen, both of whom began smoking as soon as the plane was in the air. As a nonsmoker, I found the circumstances not particularly pleasant.

My first reaction was to think, "What a dirty trick of the Devil — just when I had been peacefully situated." After a little reflection, however, I began to wonder if perhaps this was a "divine arrangement." The young man on my right responded to casual conversation, and soon we were warmly engaged in discussing a variety of topics. I felt led of the Lord to prepare the ground for sharing my faith by showing a genuine interest in him as a person and watching for

God's time to sow the seed. He was interested in glider flying, and I learned a lot about an interesting sport. I discovered he was a second-year college student, but had not yet decided on a major. I shared with him how I had changed majors several times before deciding between going into medicine or teaching biology at the college level. This led to a conversation concerning the Lord's personal interest in our lives.

My destination involved an intermediate stop. As we approached the field, our discussion was becoming very alive and seriously oriented. For a moment I was concerned that we had spent too much time talking about gliders, and he would have to leave as soon as the plane landed. I didn't feel our conversation was complete, yet the preliminary discussion seemed right in establishing a warm personal relationship. He soon informed me, however, that he was going on to my destination as well. How perfect is God's prompting when He is timing our lives!

As we continued our flight, he told me of a group of students on campus who had shared Jesus with him in a very personal and loving way. He had not felt pressured by them, and likewise appreciated our conversation together concerning the need to know the Lord as a Savior and Friend. We found we had many things in common, for his search for reality in various religions had led him to consider the Christian faith. He then accepted with genuine appreciation our little booklet, *Life's Greatest Discovery,* and we bade each other farewell. It was evident that God had carefully arranged the seating, not the Devil.

I saw again the time, love, and patience necessary to cultivate the soul that it might be ready to receive the claims of Christ. I was so grateful for the wise witness of campus friends who had prepared the young man for my added testimony. I am confident his faith is finding a clear focus in Jesus. He was familiar with Campus Crusade's "Four Spiritual Laws," and I didn't feel impressed on this occasion to press for a commitment." God was graciously drawing him to Himself. It was a privilege and a joy to be a chosen link in God's chain of love. It is a little sobering, however, to think how easily the opportunity might have been missed.

ANTICIPATE THE UNEXPECTED

There is real adventure in the Christian life. God works in both marvelous and amazing ways to accomplish His will. If we ask God to prove Himself in our desire to be a Spirit-filled witness, He will take us at our word. You may find yourself in strange places sharing with strange people at strange times, but one thing is sure—you will never be bored. *The Holy Spirit is one sure cure for boredom!* Life will never be the same for the Spirit-filled believer. Every Christian should be motivated by this overwhelming sense of divine destiny.

When opportunities come to share God's Son and His Spirit with interested inquirers, let us be careful that *this* is what we share. We can tell them how God has confirmed His Word to us personally. We *know* God's Son! We *know* God's Spirit! It is our desire to introduce them to those whom we know and love. The best way to do this is to share how real God has made His Word to us in everyday life. We have to bring heaven to earth, for this is where they are.

This may involve time and patience. We reach over to others by the bridge of love. Jesus said, "Greater love hath no man than this, that a man lay down his life for his friends." What is our life? Is it not composed of our time, energy, interests, and desires?

45

Love will give life—ours for others! As we so give of ourselves as He gave of Himself, there will come a time when the one whom God has loved through us will desire to enter into God's gifts. Our part then is to minister the Word of God in great faith and power. The Holy Spirit will always honor God's Word. This He will do regardless of time, place, or circumstances! *Real faith will never limit God.*

A short time ago we visited some Spirit-filled Episcopalian friends in a nearby town. They told us of a young friend of theirs with whom they had shared their testimony. He was planning on entering the ministry and currently was employed as a television clown on a local children's program. The Sunday of our departure, our friends called and inquired if we would like to meet the young man. He had a television program in the afternoon and was going to the church afterward to perform for the children at an ice cream social. Following this, there were further commitments for the evening. There was the possibility, however, that we could visit with him for a little while between afternoon and evening commitments.

We arrived at the church social while he was in the midst of his performance with the children. Following this, he and my friend slipped away to the rector's study where we could visit together for a time. He removed his wig and sat down. He was still dressed in his clown suit and wearing makeup in colorful patterns. It was a strange combination of events that had brought us all together under such unusual circumstances.

We shared together of the Lord's leading in all of our lives, and of our mutual desire for His full will and power in each of us. I told him of the Holy Spirit's moving among Episcopalians we had known on the West Coast, and how our own lives had been changed by God's Spirit. We carefully related our experience to God's Word and God's Son. He warmly responded to all that we said and requested that we might pray with him that he, too, might know the fullness of the Holy Spirit in his life. As we all bowed our heads in worship, we prayed that God would honor the faith in his heart and fill him with an overflowing Spirit of praise. He immediately began to worship God in a heavenly language of love. Just as we were through, the door opened and his friend arrived to take him to his next appointment!

I couldn't help but think afterward of how marvelously the eternal God can divinely order the events of time to accomplish His purposes. Furthermore, we realized as never before that God is not limited by outward appearances or circumstances. *God will meet a searching soul anywhere or anytime his faith reaches out to embrace the promises of His Word!*

WONDERFUL WORDS OF LIFE

It is also comforting to know that God is not honoring us with all our limitations but the in-living Christ and His out-spoken Word. How wise it is for us to remember from time to time that we cannot convert anyone to Christ or fill anyone with God's Spirit. This is the work and responsibility of God alone. Our part is to show openhearted and ready-minded people how to exercise their faith in God's Word so they may receive God's gifts.

The scriptural pattern for active faith is simple and sure. "*Believe* in thine heart and *confess* with thy mouth." The greatest problem is convincing people from the Scripture that the pattern is really this simple . . . there is really nothing more to do; God has done everything else!

47

Our witness should always be very Christ-centered and firmly grounded in God's Word. Begin with Jesus and end with Jesus. Relate every experience to God's Word. God always confirms His Word in experience; therefore, the two must go hand-in-hand. Satan can cause us to doubt our experiences if we don't first find them firmly rooted in God's Word. Our experience will be only as strong as our faith is firm!

Many move into the Gifts of God's Son and His Spirit and then do not move on as they should because the purpose and support from the Scriptures is lacking. It is not enough to lead others into God's gifts alone. The meaning of the gifts must be grounded in the Word and related to God's purpose for their lives.

Just recently we visited for several hours with a Lutheran pastor on the Gulf Coast. It was one of those encounters which God brings into our lives for mutual profit. We shared our testimony with him and he shared with us. As his story unfolded, we learned that he had attended a meeting in the spring where an account of the Holy Spirit's move in the historic churches was given. He went to a side room for prayer and counsel afterward. He honestly told the Lord that he wanted anything God had for him, if through it he might better serve and worship God. Someone showed him the passage in Luke 11 which promises that if we ask we shall receive. He then in faith lifted his voice and spoke forth in a heavenly language of sustained praise as the infilling Spirit gave utterance. Some time later an elderly little lady approached him and indicated she had seen in a vision a white mantle which overshadowed him as he prayed.

In spite of such almost sensational experiences, he later began to question the validity of what had happened. In fact, he finally dismissed his experience as nothing more than autosuggestion. The Lord, however, over the next few months kept bringing the matter to his attention through his reading and contacts with ministerial colleagues. A seminary professor cautioned him about depreciating any gift God might give in response to a sincere prayer of faith based on God's Word and for His glory. He also discovered that one of his colleagues had just recently entered into the same experience in the Holy Spirit. Some of this had happened just prior to our visit with him. We then shared with him how God had meaningfully related our own personal experience in the Holy Spirit to His Word and to His Son.

We visited together for some time, encouraging one another in the faith. As we parted, we both confessed God's utter faithfulness and our deep desire to worship and serve Him with every means that God's Spirit makes available to us. Devotional tongues was seen as a meaningful gift to edify us and glorify God. *True spiritual experiences will always appear both "right" and "real" when seen in the light of God's Word.*

Once again the Lord impressed upon me the necessity of grounding everything in His Holy Word. *God's Spirit will always honor God's Word to glorify God's Son.* Our experience is real because God's Word is real. The purpose of the Holy Spirit is to confirm the Living Word of God in our lives. This is our witness!

To be filled with the Holy Spirit is to be filled with power to witness!

4

Fellowship in the Spirit

The Greek New Testament word for "fellowship" (koinonia) means sharing together in and around a common interest. The English words "communion," "community," and "communicate" are derived from the same root word. It was used in the marriage contracts of that day in reference to a life that was to be shared in common by the prospective partners.

When applied to Christian fellowship, the common interest around which we are united is a person. That person is Jesus Christ! Faith in Christ as our Lord and Savior will be the basis for our future fellowship together in heaven and should be the only basis for our Christian fellowship together here on earth. *The more real the love of Jesus becomes in and through our lives, the more real our fellowship with fellow believers becomes!*

THE BASIS FOR TRUE ECUMENICITY

We are born by God's Spirit into the family of our Heavenly Father because of our life relationship with His Son and our Savior. Jesus has become our Elder Brother and we are therefore brothers and sisters to each other. We bear the same family name, and share the same glorious destiny, and are to express the same lovely life as that of our model Brother. We are united by the "life" we share in common with Him. This is the basis for a true and loving Christian community. Only an ecumenicity so born of the Spirit can ever be acceptable to our Heavenly Father.

One of the most striking and amazing characteristics of this latter-day outpouring of the Holy Spirit has been the bond of love for one another which marks real Spirit-filled believers. This Spirit of life cuts across all the barriers of peripheral doctrine and practice and links us together around Christ alone. *God has a way of mixing everybody up in His love when we submit to the harmonizing power of His Spirit.* Catholics, Episcopalians, Lutherans, Methodists, Baptists, Presbyterians, Nazarenes, Pentecostals, and a whole host of others are finding it really is possible to join together through the Holy Spirit as a family that can sing, pray, worship, and work together for Jesus.

For so long we have fenced each other out of our respective fields of Christian endeavor. We have each played in our own little spiritual "puddles" but have cautiously guarded against contamination from another. The fences have been high and the wires sharply barbed. As the latter rain of God's Spirit began to be outpoured, the pools began to enlarge. To our initial dismay and amazement, the fields of some of our rivals were receiving the same refreshing rain that at one time we had exclusively claimed as our own. Furthermore, it was apparent the edges of the expanding pools were approaching our carefully constructed fences!

That was when we made a wonderful discovery: *Man-made fences cannot hold back the rising tide of*

51

God's Spirit! In fact, as the water level rises heavenward, less and less of the fence posts can be seen. The
separate pools have long since disappeared, and there
is an awareness that this move of God's Spirit may
well "cover the whole earth as the waters cover the
sea"!

Just before we laid hands upon a Catholic young
man, who was a member of a scholastic order, for the
Holy Spirit Baptism, he requested that we first pray
for the unity which Jesus had prayed we might have.
He and another Catholic friend were very much interested in the power of the Spirit for their Christian
service, but were aware of the many differences in the
religious backgrounds of those of us who were sharing
with them. What a privilege it was to confess the
unity we had in Jesus as our Lord and Savior, and our
desire to worship Him together. We had already
sensed the bond of the Spirit which comes in genuine
fellowship around the Lord Himself. We had gathered
in His name, and He had drawn us unto Himself, and
to each other. His love leaped all the earthly barriers
which otherwise might have spoiled that holy hour.

Upon this ground of warm understanding, we
prayed that the mighty Baptizer would fill our lives
with the power of God's Holy Spirit. Together, we
submitted ourselves to His sanctifying presence. Together, we responded in faith to the infilling spirit of
worship. Together, we magnified the Lord in heavenly
tongues of praise!

Psalm 133 had become that day more than just a
lofty ideal of some misty-eyed Old Testament poet; it
was to us a genuine twentieth-century reality! May
this prophetic Psalm speak hope to all of our hearts as
once again we carefully listen to its message of life:

Behold, how good and how pleasant it is for

brethren to dwell together in unity!

It is like the precious ointment upon the head, that ran down upon the beard, even Aaron's beard: that went down to the skirts of his garments:

As the dew of Hermon, and as the dew that descended upon the mountains of Zion: for there the Lord commanded blessing, even life for evermore.

Oil is a type of the Holy Spirit. Among other things, it speaks of spiritual healing and personal consecration. Zion represents God's chosen people. The morning dew symbolizes the promises and freshness of life which envelop the lives of God's people baptized by His Spirit. The fountainhead for such spiritual ministry is our Lord Himself, high and lifted up at the right hand of God. Aaron, the first high priest, anticipates the ministry of the Lord Jesus, our Great High Priest who ever lives to make intercession for us. There is a sense in which He, too, like Aaron, received from His Father the anointing oil of consecration as He entered into His priestly ministry on our behalf after His ascension. The oil was likewise in abundant measure, for not only was His head anointed, but the oil descended downward in a mighty outpouring upon the many members which make up His earthly Body below (Acts 2:33). *What a revelation it is to realize that we all abide together in the same anointing as that of our Lord!*

One heavenly purpose for the Holy Spirit's power on earth is to unify and perfect Christ's Body, the Living Church. We are baptized into the Body of Christ when we are spiritually born into the family of our Heavenly Father. *Any construction of man that separates true brothers and sisters of God's family from fellowship with each other inflicts a wound within the*

Body of Christ and is most grievous to the Holy Spirit.
Doctrinal and traditional distinctions are occasionally
of serious importance and are not to be lightly glossed
over; yet ultimately, they will not separate us from
eternal fellowship together in heaven. Can we not anticipate such fellowship here on earth around the life
of Jesus?

As we make this our glad confession and walk in
the light of it, we shall discover how good and how
pleasant it is to dwell together in unity . . . for there
we shall experience as a family the Father's promised
blessing, even life — the altogether lovely and everlasting life of Jesus — for evermore!

We often sing with great feeling the little song,
"We are one in the Spirit, we are one in the Lord . . .
And they will know we are Christians by our love
. . . !" It may be a little song, but it has a tremendous
prophetic message. Jesus indicated that an important
witness to the world that He truly was sent of God
would be the unity of His followers (John 17:20-23).
Here are His own words expressed in His intercessory
prayer just prior to His crucifixion:

> I pray not only for these, but for those also
> who through their words will believe in me.
> May they all be one. Father, may they be one
> in us, as you are in me and I am in you, so that
> the world may believe it was you who sent me. I
> have given them the glory you gave to me, that
> they may be one as we are one.
> With me in them and you in me, may they be
> so completely one that the world will realize that
> it was you who sent me and that I have loved
> them as much as you loved me. (John 17:20-23
> JB)

This unified witness of God's love for man (Gospel) is to be worldwide in its scope and will usher in the coming of Jesus at His second advent (Matt. 24:3, 14). The disunity, suspicion, and division within Christendom has prevented the world from seriously considering the claims of Christ. Even now, however, the Holy Spirit is bringing a healing to the whole Body of Christ which ultimately is going to produce a powerful, extensive testimony concerning the claims of God's Son. *The very weapon which Satan has used to weaken the witness of the church is going to become an instrument of truth which the world cannot ignore.*

Before it is all over, nobody will be able to use the excuse, "I never had an opportunity to really see the love and life of Jesus Christ in action." *There is going to be a glorious end-time witness of God's power through an anointed army of God's people!* All will be moving as one man under the leadership of Jehovah Sabaoth (the Lord of Hosts). The Church will indeed become as an "army terrible with banners" against which the gates of hell shall not prevail.

THE FIRST CHRISTIAN COMMUNITY

How, in a practical and personal sense, do we as "living stones" find our place and purpose in this end-time expression of Christ's Church? To answer that question, let us move back through God's history book of the Church to its opening chapters. Here we can discover how the Lord chose to shape the earthly material which was to hold His heavenly treasure as "His story" in time was to unfold.

A stream at its source is usually pure, even though in character it may not have the maturity which develops along the course of future events. There was indeed a clean simplicity to the character of the first Christian community as recorded by one who was on the scene when it all began. Luke, the historian, pictures for us the adventures of these heavenly pioneers during that precarious period of the past when the entirety of God's eternal purpose rested, humanly speaking, in their hands. I am sure all heaven watched with intense interest as the breath of God's Spirit fanned the newly set fires of conversion into leaping flames of life that soon were to be seen and felt "both in Jerusalem, and in all Judaea, and in Samaria and unto the uttermost part of the earth!" (Acts 1:8). Here is the story in Saint Luke's own words of how this remarkable fellowship was first started:

When they heard this [Peter's Pentecost sermon], they were cut to the quick, and they cried out to Peter and the other apostles, "Men and fellow Jews, what shall we do now?" Peter told them, "You must repent and every one of you must be baptized in the name of Jesus Christ, so that you may have your sins forgiven and receive the gift of the Holy Spirit. . . ."

Then those who welcomed his [Peter's] message were baptized, and on that day alone about three thousand souls were added to the number of disciples. They continued steadily learning the teaching of the apostles, and joined in their fellowship, in the breaking of bread, and in prayer.

Everyone felt a deep sense of awe while many miracles and signs took place through the apostles. All the believers shared everything in common; they sold their possessions and goods and divided the proceeds among the fellowship according to individual need.

Day after day they met by common consent in the Temple; they broke bread together in their homes, sharing meals with simple joy. They praised God continually and all the people respected them. Every day the Lord added to their number those who were finding salvation. (Acts 2:37-38; 41-47 Phillips)

From this account, it is apparent that following water and Holy Spirit Baptism, new converts were immediately introduced into the corporate life of the newly established Christian community. There they found and steadfastly maintained their place in the Lord.

It was a place of instruction, fellowship, and prayer. It was a place of power, praise, and holy wonder. It was a place of work, worship, and witness. It was a place of love, joy, and peace.

The community was characterized by God's love, which is far more than a soft, sentimental feeling. It was evidenced by sacrifice and sharing; on occasion, by kindly correction, or, if necessary, even firm discipline (Acts 5:1-11). It was the kind of love that was not blind to faults, but could keep on loving anyway. It was the oil of God's Spirit which kept the community sweet, even though the inevitable frictions of one life rubbing against another became evident (Acts 6:1). It was a ground from which the fruit of the Spirit could grow as "togetherness" became practical and real.

In his epistles, Paul defines some of the many ministries which the Lord Himself has personally and purposely placed within the Christian community:

And His gifts were varied; He Himself appointed and gave men to us, some to be apostles, some prophets, some evangelists, some pastors and teachers . . . . Others were given to us to be practical servants and assistants, personal sources of encouragement and exhortation, gener-

57

ous givers with sincerity, diligent leaders and administrators, "glad angels of mercy" and miracle and wonder-workers. (Eph. 4:11; Rom. 12:6-8; I Cor. 12:28-29 various translations)

A "steadfastness" of character developed in the first Christian community as God prepared them for a time of persecution and dispersal which undoubtedly was inconceivable in the earlier days of their fellowship. God compressed much into their lives in those few short months of sharing together in His Spirit. Little did they know of the unexpected opportunities that soon would be forced upon them. But God knew! When the time of displacement came, they were ready to "risk the glorious and reap the miraculous." And they did!

The following account is found in Acts 8:1-8 (TLG):

Saul was in complete agreement with the killing of Stephen. Beginning that day a great wave of persecution swept over the church in Jerusalem, and everyone except the apostles fled into Judea and Samaria. . . .

Saul was like a wild man, going everywhere to devastate the believers, even entering private homes and dragging out men and women alike and jailing them. But the believers who had fled Jerusalem went everywhere preaching the Good News about Jesus!

Philip, for instance, went to the city of Samaria and told the people there about Christ. Crowds listened intently to what he had to say, because of the miracles he did. Many evil spirits were cast out, screaming as they left their victims, and many who were paralyzed or lame were healed. So there was much joy in that city!

Who knows how very important our community life in the Spirit may be in our day and age? How very little we, too, see of the future in any sure or predictable way. What a comfort it is to know God always prepares His people as they find their place in the fellowship of the faithful. What renewed interest becomes ours in recognizing the power and purpose God has placed in His holy Church. We will wish to pursue this further in both a practical and personal way.

The simplest expression of the Church is where two or three are gathered together in Jesus' name. He has promised to be there in the midst of them (Matt. 18:20). As we have seen, it is only through the Body of Christ or fellowship of believers that God's *full* glory can be manifested to the world. It is only through the fellowship of *many* believers that God's manifold expressions of beauty and power can be *fully* revealed. We each have an integral part of that power and beauty through the gifts and graces, but we need one another to make the divine picture complete. There are no free-lancers in God's economy! We all need the spiritual ministries of one another if we are to fulfill God's full will.

The new power which God desires to progressively release through the lives of Spirit-filled believers should be channeled back into one's local church! It is suggested that unless God leads otherwise, one should share his Pentecostal experience in the Holy Spirit with his pastor. Carefully explain how real Jesus Christ has become to your life and your deep desire to glorify Him in ways of Christian love. Assure your pastor, if he seems unduly concerned, that anytime he might feel it would be desirable, you will be happy to quietly withdraw in Christian love; but until then you feel your place is in the fellowship of the church. This will place a responsibility upon you to live a Christ-honoring life. It will also place the responsibility for any possible separation in fellowship upon others.

Real truth needs no defense; it will authenticate itself! One need never feel he has to defend himself or God. All we are required to do is to manifest Jesus Christ through our lives by His Spirit. We can always be ready to share the Gifts of God's Son and His Spirit with others as He provides the opportunity, but never is there any occasion for argument. This does not mean that there will not be opposition. The real test of brokenness before the Lord may come during times of unfair criticism and even persecution. Purpose in your heart to follow your Lord whatever the cost. There is no sweeter reward in all of life than to know you are in the center of His will, and God's will is Jesus, simply Jesus.

FELLOWSHIP: A DIVINE IMPERATIVE

It is also imperative to find fellowship with other Spirit-filled believers if you are going to grow in the full purpose for which He has called you by His Spirit. As we have learned, there is the need to be further grounded in the Word as it is broken in Christian fellowship. You will also find that you have brothers and sisters who are going, or have gone, through the same valleys of possible doubts and discouragement which you may be facing. Furthermore, oftentimes our needs, whether physical or spiritual, may be met through the ministry of all the spiritual gifts (I Cor. 12:8-10). The very purpose of God's good gifts is to edify the Body and glorify the Head who is Jesus. You are an important part of the Body and in living union with the Head.

Also, as we grow in our spiritual life, we shall find God sovereignly prompting us to move out by faith into the exercise of some of the spiritual gifts. As your own ministry develops, you may find in God's grace that you are "excelling" more in some gifts than in others to the benefit of fellow believers. To learn and to grow with others is a mutually profitable experience.

Without Christian fellowship with Spirit-filled believers, all too often the faithless influence of others concerning the significance of His spiritual gifts will darken our sense of bright expectation. Once our faith is so dampened, the streams of God's Spirit in new and powerful ways will slacken, and we will find ourselves back in a "life as usual" sort of an existence. *Those who move in and "move on" nearly always are those who have continued to sharpen their newfound spiritual experience in warm Christian fellowship!*

We just have not been created to "go it alone"! A sustained lack of fellowship will almost always quench even the brightest flame of God's Spirit in a life. We need one another! God has admonished us in His Word to forsake not the assembling of ourselves together but to exhort and encourage one another all the more as we see the day approaching (Heb. 10:25).

Follow that prompting of God's Spirit for spiritual fellowship! Actually, Christian fellowship is the natural outcome and desire of an overflowing life in the Spirit. Go with an expectation of both sharing and receiving. Paul's pattern for a Spirit-filled meeting is that each participant should have a hymn, or a teaching, or a revelation, or an utterance in an unknown tongue, or an interpretation of it. "[But] let everything be constructive and edifying and for the good of all" (I Cor. 14:26, TAB).

We have experienced many times of fellowship in home prayer-and-share meetings that have followed this scriptural pattern. We have seen God's Spirit through His servants and by His gifts manifest God's Son in marvelous ways. There have been times of soul-searching and correction. There have been occasions of tenderness of God's Spirit sweetly moved across the hearts of sensitive believers. At other times, the whole group has joined in beautiful songs in the Spirit where both words and music were of a heavenly nature. Here is true worship in the beauty of holiness. Sometimes God would move powerfully and in spectacular ways to bring physical deliverance and healing. Perhaps after the ministry of God's Word, the Holy Spirit would bring meaningful confirmation to hearts and minds through prophecy or tongues and interpretation.

Often those who lack faith to receive the Holy Spirit in His fullness by themselves will find in the faith and wisdom of other Spirit-filled believers all the added encouragement that is needed. *Fellowship builds faith!*

The ways of God's choosing for meeting the needs of His people are unpredictable for any given meeting. His purpose, however, is always the same: to encourage, strengthen and quicken the believers, and magnify His Son—*to edify the Body and glorify the Head.* This is the fundamental principle for Christian fellowship of any kind. Every participant should be governed by this rule. The Holy Spirit will *always* honor with His manifest Presence *every* meeting that is so centered in God's Son. This is God's pattern for His people.

Real fellowship will follow through in real life. The consequence of sharing Jesus with fellow believers is a desire to also share Him with unbelievers. "That which we have seen and heard declare we unto you, that ye also may have fellowship with us: and truly our fellowship is with the Father, and with His Son Jesus Christ" (I John 1:3). The Body of Christ possesses *Life.* "Life begets Life!" Once we have experienced real *Life* there is an overwhelming desire to share it with others. Basically, that is what real spiritual fellowship is: the sharing of this *Life*. Jesus said, "I am . . . the life." Fellowship is simply sharing Jesus!

To be filled with the Spirit is to be filled with a desire to share the life of Jesus with one another!

5

The Spirit-Filled Home

Six times over, God declared that His creation in the beginning was good in His sight. His seventh observation concludes with the startling statement that a situation existed which was not good in the light of His eternal purpose. "It is not good that man should dwell alone; I will make a help meet for him." *The desire of our Heavenly Father has always been to have a family to and through which His life and love could be expressed.*

Eternal purpose had been born into the heart of Adam, and in vain he sought for some expression in the beautiful array of living things which God had created that could complete his life—something that would relate to the unfulfilled sense of destiny which made him restless within. He had been created to share God's love with another, and that someone was not to be found. We can almost feel the sense of sadness and personal disappointment which were Adam's in that early morning hour of creation when he faced the wonder of a whole new world . . . alone!

There is a touch of pathos climaxed with joy as one reads the record of the events which surrounded the very first marriage that God ever made:

> So the Lord God formed from the soil every
> kind of animal and bird, and brought them to the
> man to see what he would call them; and whatev-
> er he called them, that was their proper name.
> But still there was no proper helper for the man.
> Then the Lord God caused the man to fall
> into a deep sleep, and took one of his ribs and
> closed up the place from which He had removed
> it, and made the rib into a woman, and brought
> her to the man.
> "This is it!" Adam exclaimed. "She is a part
> of my own bone and flesh! Her name is 'woman'
> because she was taken out of a man." This ex-
> plains why a man leaves his father and mother
> and is joined to his wife in such a way that the
> two become one person. (Gen. 2:19-24 TLB)

God, Himself, established the first family in the
history of mankind. Immediately, the Adversary appeared in an attempt to frustrate at the very outset
God's plan for and through His people. The seed of
death was sown in the heart of a man, and Satan
would have succeeded in a tragic, timeless way if it
had not been for another home, some thousands of
years later, into which the Savior of the world was to
come. And come He did! God is still going to have a
people, and His plan shall yet succeed. *Jesus is indeed
the firstborn of a family of many sons and daughters,
all of whom will joyfully acknowledge God as their
Heavenly Father and Jesus as their Elder Brother.*
Satan is a hard loser and still is striking at the
home, both Christian and non-Christian, in a frantic
display of his wrath as he sees his final hour approaching. The family unit represents the simplest expres-

65

sion of the Living Church in action! Jesus said that where two or three are gathered together in His name, there He would be to honor our confessions of faith to our Father (Matt. 18:18-20).

The Enemy especially recognizes the power and authority which the Spirit-filled home can generate, and He does not remain idle in view of this. It is encouraging that wherever the Adversary comes in like a flood, God has promised to raise up a standard against him (Isa. 59:19). This is precisely the picture which we have found at the level of the home and family wherever we have gone in our ministry for the Lord. Many lessons have been learned, and God has repeatedly emphasized the importance of the truth which we shall shortly share together. All of it has been born out of experience and relates in a most practical way to one of the most important centers of both spiritual conflict and promised blessing.

Basically, the relationship of marriage and the family is one of sharing together in life. In God's divine order, this begins at the level of our life in Christ. It is only as a husband and wife become spiritually alive together in Him that God's full purpose can be achieved through their lives as He intended. Consequently, the apostle Paul gets a running start on his discussion concerning the Christian home by first encouraging the Ephesian believers to ever be filled to overflowing with the Holy Spirit. He then identifies some of these streams as the rivers of praise, joy, and thanksgiving. The last stream he considers is one which is not often emphasized among the fruit of the Spirit. *It is the stream of mutual submission!* (Eph. 5:18-21).

There is a spiritual principle behind our learning to submit to and thereby share the life of Jesus in and with each other. It is the cornerstone of truth upon which God is going to build His Triumphant Church! The greater is usually gained at the level of the lesser. It is as we learn to live together with each other at the level of the home that we will learn to witness and worship together as members of God's greater family. The everyday life and problems of the home become the earthly ground from which the fruit of the Spirit can most effectively grow. The Holy Spirit is a very practical person who desires to bring practical answers to practical problems. Let us see how this works out in real life.

We will wish to consider first of all some of the practical aspects that relate to a home where all members are filled with the Spirit and desire to move on with God. We also will want to face situations which are less than ideal; where one or more members don't really know Jesus as the Savior, or, if they do, are disinterested or antagonistic to some aspects of Holy Spirit Baptism.

Let us begin by considering some simple but basic concepts concerning the various phases of ministry which are related to a Christian marriage. Throughout our entire discussion, we will be interested in spiritual principles which will minister life. To fall into a legal attitude will only bring frustration and eventually death, spiritually speaking. The words that God would speak to us are Spirit and they are life! (John 6:63).

THE THREEFOLD MINISTRY OF THE SPIRIT-FILLED HUSBAND AND WIFE

There is a threefold spiritual ministry which God has ordained for every Christian couple. *The first area of ministry is to each other in mutual edification and encouragement.* This involves praying and sharing together in God's Word. This is a very practical way of keeping communication lines clear at other levels. The Lord holds our unity in His Spirit as supremely important.

The second area involves their ministry together as parents within the home, and also their witness as a couple to the world without. Jesus teamed His disciples in twos and then sent them forth with the authority of His name. There are some things a man and wife (and father and mother) can accomplish as a team which could be achieved in no other way.

The third area of ministry involves that which is personally unique. A wife and mother has spiritual responsibilities and privileges which are distinctively and specifically hers. This same is true of a husband and father. Again, this will involve opportunities both inside and outside the home situation. Every person has a particular place and a divinely ordained function in the Body of Christ which never should be depreciated or suppressed.

The distinct character of the threefold ministries is to be recognized and appreciated by both marriage partners. It is their privilege to encourage each other to excel in the gifts and graces which will enable them to express the life of Jesus in all of these areas of spiritual responsibility. As we shall see, where these three ministries are not appreciated and related to each other, serious problems can arise.

SHARING TOGETHER
IN THE LIFE OF JESUS

Before considering the specific roles of husband and wife in the Christian home, it would be well to consider the unity of spirit and harmony of heart which can be achieved only as we learn to share together in the life of Jesus. God desires that our communication with Him and with each other be carefully guarded as something that is most precious in His sight. An openness in love is the best remedy for hidden, festering resentments. Something as simple as daily devotions *together* can help us keep short accounts with each other and the Lord if Jesus is truly welcome in our midst. It is difficult to hold a hurt or a grudge in our heart and pray in the Spirit together at the same time. *The convicting power of the Holy Spirit will consistently crowd us to the cross for forgiveness!*

The Lord taught my wife and me the significance of sharing together in Jesus even before we were married. The Holy Spirit is a marvelous marriage-maker, and, I discovered, a very clever and effective cupid. We both, unknown to each other, had arrived at a point of commitment to Christ which involved God's will in every area of our lives.

One Sunday afternoon in my dormitory room at Rice University, where I was taking my graduate training, I prayed that I might find a companion who was going the same way with God—as I had recently found Him—that we might go with Him together. My future wife had recently discovered the Lord in a new and personal way and had likewise submitted to His will concerning the possibility of marriage and a Christian home. To shorten the story, for the Lord had several hurdles in the natural to overcome (one of which was my timidity), we found each other that very night after the evening church service. It was a rather rapid and remarkable answer to prayer. That was in the fall; the following June we were married!

As mentioned above, God began to teach us the significance of sharing together in Him. Before our marriage, I would call her every evening, and then, upon returning to my room, would have my time of devotions. At the same time, she was also reading and praying, so we sensed a togetherness in our worship with the Lord. Consequently, it was the most natural thing from the very first day of our marriage to continue our daily devotions together and to honor His presence in the usual problems and concerns of early homemaking.

The years have now passed and our prayer together goes beyond just the "devotional time," and involves the Lord in our conversation anytime we feel the need and desire to recognize and confess His wisdom and power. We often pray as we travel along the freeways, allowing God to make the car a holy altar on wheels. *Any place is holy where Jesus is!* This may seem to be a rather simple theme, but I have discovered in counseling with many who are facing marriage problems, that sharing together with Jesus in prayer is a missing dimension in their home, It can also be the beginning of a genuine healing in their lives.

Harmony in the home is based upon a unity of the Spirit which brings a oneness of heart and mind. God places a supreme value upon our "togetherness" in Him. Some years ago, when the Holy Spirit was freshly moving among the historic churches on the West Coast, the Lord taught my wife and me an important lesson concerning our unity in the Spirit. I had been going to meetings of all sorts, even on short notice, as if God's entire plan of the ages rested upon my shoulders alone. My wife had been very patient and understanding concerning my great zeal in the Lord, even though on some occasions my decision to go somewhere was more in terms of an announcement than it was a matter of mutual prayer and agreement.

It all came to a crisis one evening when I cautiously informed my wife of another important meeting which I felt it necessary to support with my presence. I could tell from the back of her head the idea hadn't set too well, but since a visiting student was helping her do the dinner dishes, she didn't voice her contrary feelings. I took advantage of the opportunity and slipped away, confessing bravely to the Lord that even though family and friends might misunderstand, still I would be true to "my ministry" for His Kingdom. The meeting wasn't as important as I had thought it would be, but one never knows when God might break through in some spectacular way, and if He did, I was pretty sure He would want my help!

When I arrived home, my wife was more distressed than I had ever seen her in all our married life. I realized I had not taken her concern and feelings as seriously as I would have, had I been more sensitive to God's Spirit. The Lord was faithful in the midst of it all, however, and impressed us to rest in Him for the night and discuss the situation together in the morning. We also sensed there was something about which he wished to deal with us.

After breakfast the next day we submitted ourselves to the Lord and to each other with open and humble hearts. I realized my zeal for God had assumed a strong, striving spirit which had pushed me into the area of pride. My wife recognized that her resentment had not been brought to the cross for His inner work of redeeming grace. But more than this, God, Himself, revealed His mind to us concerning the basic problem.

We were assured that in times of disagreement, His primary concern was not with who was right or wrong, but rather with why our unity in His Spirit had been broken. The next order of the day was not the decision we had considered so important, but a restoration of our communion in Christ. Sometimes this would mean giving up our respective positions to the Lord, realizing He would return to us *both* whatever was truly His will and pleasure; there might even be an alternative which the Holy Spirit was waiting to reveal.

Such mutual submission to Jesus and each other is not always easy when everything natural within our lives is geared for conflict. But the baptizing power of Jesus can release us from ourselves, if we are willing and obedient. There is no sweeter victory in all the world than to see Satan yield to the authority which God has invested in those who purpose to dwell together in unity through the power of His Spirit. My wife and I have subsequently had many opportunities to prove the wisdom of God's instruction for us. We both can confess with real conviction, based on experience, that the working power of the Holy Spirit is most effective in very practical ways!

THE ROLE OF THE SPIRIT-FILLED HUSBAND

For the husband is the head of the wife, even as as Christ is the head of the church. . . . Husbands love your wives, even as Christ also loved the church, and gave himself for it; That He might sanctify and cleanse it . . . [and] present it to himself a glorious church, not having spot, or wrinkle, or any such thing. (Eph. 5:23, 25-27)

Husbands, live with your wives with understanding and consideration, honoring them as the weaker vessel, and as being heirs together, sharing in the grace of life; that your prayers may not be hindered (I Pet. 3:7 various translations).

These and other Scriptures make it very clear that

72

God has given a priestly ministry to the husband as the head of the home. The Lord holds him primarily responsible for the spiritual welfare of the family. With this responsibility, the Lord provides both divine authority and power to graciously fulfill every related obligation. This would be impossible apart from the gifts and graces of the Holy Spirit which lift us beyond our natural limitations.

The husband is not only responsible before the Lord to excel in his own unique ministry in the family of God, but he is to appreciate and encourage the personal ministry which belongs to his wife. This would involve reassurance, on some occasions, protection, and even spiritual counsel, should such direction appear advisable. Never is his authority to be harsh or heavy-handed, but rather a blessing as is the Lordship of Jesus.

I asked a very successful businessman who was really the spiritual leader in his home. After some hesitation, he confessed he had relegated this role to his wife, who, besides being a very strong personality, was a very gifted woman with an outstanding ministry in the Spirit. He explained further that she spent hours in prayer and study, and his business obligations prevented him from delving as deeply as she did into spiritual things. Consequently, he had yielded this responsibility to her. He had rationalized his role as merely providing for her material welfare and thereby supporting her ministry for the Lord.

Sadly, he had failed to realize that the God of eternity does not always measure spirituality in terms of clock hours. Furthermore, God always provides the spiritual gifts necessary for his divinely appointed responsibilities. The spiritual disorder in their home was reflected in other members of their family who, likewise, had submitted to a definite, dominating influence that characterized her life. Some of the scars were painfully deep.

Strong spiritual ministries of women which overshadow the authority of their husbands in the home have a tendency to influence other women in a similar way. To willfully ignore divinely instituted leadership can lead only to disorder and limitation in God's greater family as well. How very much the loving authority and guiding wisdom of this husband was needed in his home! What a greater blessing his wife could have been in the Body of Christ if he had accepted his God-given priestly ministry for the family. One also wonders if there wasn't a latent ministry which was uniquely his that has remained undeveloped because somewhere along the line, business interests were substituted for spiritual responsibility!

Some husbands, on the other hand, assume a position of rightful authority, but without the tenderness that characterizes the Christlike life. It is possible for even gifted men of God to be less than gracious in the home. I have seen husbands humiliate their wives in front of others by depreciating remarks which were devastating in effect. Jesus did not come to destroy, but to heal and make people whole. *Love is kind and courteous!*

One should never exert a dominating influence upon the life of another to the extent that he no longer feels worthwhile as an individual. It is a serious thing to suppress the soul of those whom God desires to free. The baptizing power of Jesus should bring a glorious release in the Spirit to every member in the home in very practical ways. Being "heirs together in the grace of life" involves time as well as eternity. How beautiful it is when a husband and wife respect each other and together make decisions in the Lord concerning such practical things as family finances and thereby bring a heavenly quality to earthly affairs!

"Christ so loved the church that He gave Himself for her. . . ." There is another dimension to the love of a truly Spirit-filled husband for his wife if it is truly to be

74

Christlike in quality. It involves a willingness to be first in submitting to the cross of self-denial when it is necessary to bridge the communication gap that disagreement can bring. "Communion" and "communication" come from the same Greek root word, which also includes the concept of fellowship.

When the spiritual fellowship is broken between a man and his wife, there is also a breach in their communion with the Lord. This is a grievous wound to the Body of Christ, and only the unifying ministry of the cross can heal the stripe so carelessly inflicted upon His back. *Usually we are so concerned about our own hurt feelings that we fail to think of the pain this brings to the Lord!* No wonder the Scriptures speak of the Spirit as being grieved by such behavior (Eph. 4:30 — note the context!).

When personal disagreements develop to the point that our communion in the Spirit is spoiled and a stubborn stalemate is the result, only the cross can restore our fellowship in the Lord. Furthermore, God expects the husband, as the head of the home, in Christlike love to go to the cross first! This is easier said than done, but the purpose of the Holy Spirit is to give to us the power to do a right thing whether we feel like it or not.

"Going to the cross" means dying to our pride and self-pity and apologizing for a spoiled attitude of heart and mind. The inner approval of the Holy Spirit will come *after* we make our decision and as we follow through, not before. An attitude of humility in one heart will tend to reproduce itself in the life of another, and then the problem, which was inflated as our egos, likewise collapses to its realistic size. Now God's word of wisdom can find the spiritual soil necessary for its reception and solution-producing life. (As the reader probably has already assumed, the author is writing from some rather practical, personal

experiences. Again, one can say most emphatically —
it really does work! I must admit, however, that on
some occasions my wife has out-raced me to the cross.
The important thing is that we both finally arrived!)

THE ROLE OF THE SPIRIT-FILLED WIFE

And the Lord God said, It is not good that man
should be alone; I will make him an help meet for
him. (Gen. 2:18)

Wives, submit yourselves unto your own husbands, as unto the Lord (Eph. 5:22).

See to it that you deeply respect your husband
— obeying, praising and honoring him; and defer-
ring to him and loving and admiring him exceeding-
ly. (Eph. 5:33 various translations)

As the husband assumes his role, it will not be difficult for the Spirit-filled wife to accept with appreciation
her role as clearly outlined in the Scriptures above. A
husband cannot truly be the whole man God intended for
him to be apart from his wife. Likewise, a wife actually
cannot find and fulfill her own life apart from the ministry of her husband. She will discover her real destiny as
divinely ordained only as she submits to the headship of
her husband in the home.

*Strong-souled women who usurp the spiritual lead-
ership in the family will ultimately reap great limitation
in terms of God's holy purposes!* Such situations often
develop where the wife is filled with the Spirit first and
then moves rapidly into revelation, prophecy, and other
gifts. The husband is directly or indirectly shamed for
not keeping pace with his wife and consequently either
submits to her seeming spiritual superiority, or shuns the
whole scene and endeavors to salvage his ego by excelling
in some secular activity such as his business.

76

Very often wives in similar situations gravitate to each other and develop strong, dominating ministries which can isolate other wives from their husbands as well. Often such meetings become mystical and are prone to error. There is an emphasis on special revelations which lead to self-exaltation and isolation from the Body of Christ as a whole. (Although there may be an emphasis on Jesus in a mystical sense, it is in a way which relieves them from any practical control outside the privileged group.) Usually individuals so involved are most unsubmissive to even kindly correction and justify their position on the basis of having pressed through to "deeper truth" which cannot be fully appreciated by those "less sensitive" to the Spirit.

Such deviations from wholesome Christian fellowship are not limited to women's groups by any means, but the latter are perhaps particularly prone to such deception, if those involved willfully ignore the principles of spiritual leadership in their own home. Had Eve submitted to the headship of Adam and patiently waited, until together they could discern the truth concerning the first temptation, the story might have ended quite differently! The apostle Paul indicates it wasn't Adam who was deceived (not that he was immune), but rather Eve who was deluded and fell into sin (I Tim. 2:14).

Sensitivity to the Spirit-world, coupled with a rather emotional nature, needs the balance of that stability which wisdom and God-given understanding can bring. The latter ministries of the Spirit are not as sensational or spectacular as some of the other gifts, but are absolutely necessary to maintain a straight path. *How very much we need each other in the Body of Christ!*

The author in his travels across the nation has seen the tragic results which follow the temptation to be free from all spiritual restraint, which God's divine order for the home wisely and graciously provides. The danger cannot be overemphasized, but must be seen in the safety of the Lord's divine plan.

A lady was determined to visit a noted healing evangelist, for she was convinced through special revelation that she, too, was gifted. It became my responsibility to respond to her questions in a personal interview. Her husband came with her, but was very mild and soft-spoken. She answered most of the questions which I directed toward him. We soon centered our conversation around Jesus, however, and they both warmly responded, and we became better acquainted. The picture soon became clear. Her claims to revelations and special gifts had elevated her to a place of spiritual leadership in the home. Emotionally, she was not capable of handling the responsibilities involved. Finally, I spoke rather forthrightly, explaining to her how much she really needed her husband's quiet counsel and stability. She was so tense I wasn't sure how much was actually registering, but her husband seemed to respond.

After a time, it became apparent that neither had been baptized by Jesus in the full sense of the experience. Both expressed a desire for all God wanted for them and requested prayer. I indicated I first would pray with her husband, since he was to be the priest in their home. He immediately and restfully responded with a most fluent expression of heavenly praise in tongues. The peace on his face spoke of a simple, relaxed relationship with Jesus which their home desperately required.

We then prayed for her, but she wasn't able to find a full release in the Lord, so intent had she been in her previous struggle for recognition. Hopefully, her husband assumed his rightful role in the days that followed and encouraged her desire to serve the Lord in a more restful and gracious way. His ministry to her was more needed than either of them realized.

On another occasion, my wife invited a visiting student to share with me a spiritual concern which they had discussed, involving her former experiences. She was in her middle twenties and had recently been released by the Lord from a rather unpleasant past. She had been accepted into a Christian home along with several other girls with the purpose of getting stabilized in their newfound life in Christ. Two gifted women had established the ministry as a means of encouraging young ladies who needed to be grounded in God before assuming the responsibility of facing the world on their own.

Both of the women in charge were greatly gifted along the lines of revelation, prophecy, and deliverance. What began so graciously, however, became a source of great spiritual distress. The atmosphere of love and kindness could become harsh and psychologically cruel if either of the two women was crossed. The "gifts" were used to establish their authority, and anyone who refused to submit was directly or indirectly threatened with divine punishment!

The student had left, in spite of warnings that she was out of the Lord's will and would suffer God's judgment. It was with fear that she went, but once apart from the dark and dominating influence of the two women, she was reassured by the peace of the Lord. I inquired about the husbands of the women, and as might be anticipated, neither of them was the spiritual leader of his home. Once again, we saw a meaningful ministry which had drifted into error because God's divine order for the family had been ignored.

There are beautiful and lovely stories to share as well, for the Holy Spirit will honor God's Word in most marvelous ways when we accept its principles for our own lives. The following testimony was written by a wife and mother in the Midwest who decided to hold to God's principles and claim His promises:

After receiving the Baptism in the Holy Spirit, my one desire was that my family would also share this dimension of reality, and that we truly be one in the Spirit. For me, it had to be more than just the testimony of my words. I wanted them to see something in my life that they wanted!

The desire to "give every man a reason for the hope that was within me" drove me to the Word, for this is what He promises to watch over and perform. When the Enemy sought to divide or make me think I must press ahead alone, the Holy Spirit would remind me, "Of one flesh hath He made you, called according to His purposes." I also saw in the Word that the husband is head of the wife, so I sought God to bring Paul (my husband) forth as the spiritual head of the household. . . .

That winter he joined a study group on the Holy Spirit and subsequently received the Baptism himself at a service where Harald Bredesen ministered.

As the Lord caused me to accept leadership in Bible studies and prayer groups, He also has quietly reminded me in regard to my husband, "He must increase, and I must decrease," even as with my Lord. How faithful He has been! First, He gave my husband a sixth-grade Sunday school class to teach and with which to grow. Paul then started a noon Bible study at his office, which has prospered for three years and has given a real outlet for sharing. In the evening groups, we all share together and each has something to contribute which no other can. . . .

It is so very practical to recognize that nothing just happens; that our steps are ordered of the Lord. Consequently, we look for His purpose in everything! God provided us with a mountain home, but we were led to finish the interior ourselves. As a result, unsaved men from my husband's office have graciously offered help, along with our Spirit-filled friends, and we have observed the Holy Spirit drawing them to Jesus and ministering to all in a natural, spontaneous way.

Another lady, who was greatly used in a teaching ministry to women, extended her faith to claim her unsaved husband as the head of her home. She never accepted a speaking engagement unless he was agreeable. Her requests were reasonable, and he never refused. One evening, however, he did express his preference for her to remain at home. At first she stiffened in resentment, but quickly reaffirmed her commitment to honor her husband's desires in this area as from the Lord. To her consolation, she later learned the nature of the meeting would have placed her in a very unpleasant and embarrassing position. How grateful she was that God had chosen this means of both sparing her personal discomfort and simultaneously confirming her commitment!

To claim one's mate by faith as *already* in God's chosen place of responsibility and wherever possible, as prompted by the Spirit, to seek his counsel and advice will often help maintain a restful atmosphere in the home. If we strive in a soulish way to move our mates to the Lord, either as Savior or Baptizer, we shall only succeed in hindering the pursuing power of the Holy Spirit. I recall a wife who, in a spirit of disappointment almost bordering on disdain, described how far short her husband was from her ideal of a spiritual leader. One could almost detect a little bit of pride in her impatience. None of these qualities speak of the winsome graces that can attract a person to the Lord. I suggested that instead of continually confessing what was wrong with her husband, she should see him as God desires him to become and wherever possible begin responding to him as the head of the house.

If we don't see by faith our loved ones in the healing hands of Jesus, we will start pushing them around with our own! I did this with my wife in regard to the Baptism in the Holy Spirit. We had been moving together in our walk with the Lord until I was filled with the Spirit as described earlier. I then began to pressure her psychologically to attend all kinds of meetings, so she, too, might meet the "gentle dove" of God's Spirit. She reacted so emphatically that after a couple of weeks I gave up in sheer despair.

The day she did receive her Baptism in the Holy Spirit, I recall telling someone how blue and discouraged I was. I finally had concluded that if she was ever going to be filled with the Holy Spirit, God was going to have to do it! I had decided I was going to take my hands off completely and leave the matter totally up to the Lord. That night she voluntarily suggested we go to a home prayer meeting where a man mightily used of God was going to speak. The whole evening was practically dead until shortly before 10:00 P.M. The Spirit of God then moved in prophecy indicating His desire that we seek His face in prayer. With great expectation, everyone headed for a place to pray.

We had a newborn baby just a few weeks old, and about 10:00 P.M. my wife always became restless and wanted to return home. I would usually try to pressure her to stay at the meetings a little longer. This evening, however, as much as I wanted to stay for her sake, I decided I was really going to keep my commitment to God not to interfere. I even went so far as to approach her first to suggest perhaps we might want to go home to the baby. I was about to speak when she went by me like I wasn't there — heading for a green sofa on the other side of the room.

She knelt and immediately began to pray that God would fill her with His Holy Spirit. I felt I didn't have to hold back any longer, and I remember I fell all over myself getting the visiting evangelist to her side. I was so excited he couldn't understand me at first. Needless to say, this was all God had been waiting for . . . for me to get out of the way! She was beautifully baptized in the Holy Spirit to our mutual joy that very hour.

My wife has ministered encouragement to me in many more ways than I can tell. There are times when her discernment has been more sensitive than mine, and we are learning to carefully listen to God's voice together. She has a disarming way of quoting my own words when God is prompting me to practice what I preach! I can personally testify that one of the most precious gifts the Lord can give a man is a companion with whom the wonderful adventure of the Spirit-filled life can be shared.

THE ROLES OF SPIRIT-FILLED PARENTS AND CHILDREN

Fathers, do not rouse your children to resentment, but rear them tenderly in the training, discipline and counsel of the Lord. (Eph. 6:4 various translations)

Children, obey your parents in the Lord: for this is right. Honour thy father and thy mother; which is the first commandment with promise;

that it may be well with thee, and thou mayest live long on the earth. (Eph. 6:1-3)

The Lord impressed me once that I was to be as patient and long-suffering with my children as He was with me! The love of God is neither blind nor sentimental. It often involves both discipline and direction, but within the context of faith, hope, and understanding. Divine love is powerfully persistent, yet graciously tempered with tender mercy and humility (I Cor. 13:4-7; I Pet. 3:8-9).

It takes the power of the Holy Spirit Himself to translate such a lofty ideal into an earthly reality. Once again we appreciate the admonition of the apostle Paul, that we ever be filled with the Holy Spirit. There is no alternative by which a heavenly harmony can come to our homes. Where else might there be a greater need in a very practical way for the power which only the fruit and gifts of the Spirit can bring?

As our own children entered into their teenage years, many of the usual problems of communication and understanding began to develop. I have learned many life principles concerning my own relationship with my Heavenly Father and other members of His family through experiences with my own family. Often the discipline of His hand rested heavily upon me as I would seek to solve family problems (all of which have spiritual centers) in a strong, self-willed way.

God dealt with me in my need to trust both my children and His Spirit concerning the temptations which every teenager must face. There is a sense in which it is better to have trusted our children and have been disappointed for a time than not to have trusted them when we should have. This does not mean we can be careless or unconcerned about our responsibilities relative to their companions and activities. But, God would have us stand with Him in a strong faith concerning His keeping and protecting power. *The Lord once reproved me for always picturing my children in the hands of the Devil, rather than in the hands of Jesus!* My faithless attitude resulted in harsh and heavy-handed endeavors to line out their lives without the courtesy of including their feelings in my decisions. I forced my will, but lost their love and respect!

The Lord in His grace began to show me the importance of recognizing their growing need to become individuals whose spiritual dignity was to be respected. Their responsibility to God was becoming something direct and personal, rather than secondhand relationship through their parents. This meant giving them enough freedom, within defined limits, to make mistakes while still within a family environment of redeeming love.

The shifting of our confidence from natural parental discipline to that of the Spirit for the children involved some painful episodes. I, especially, was slow to completely trust God's work in their lives and repeatedly interfered with my own endeavors which were often motivated by a strong, proud spirit. There were even times when I threatened them with the "judgement of God", if I felt I wasn't eliciting the quality of repentance which I thought was appropriate! More than once the Holy Spirit so severely convicted me of my un-Christlike attitude and actions, that I was required to apologize for facing a problem with them in a way that had displeased God.

It is so easy in the interaction of personalities for one wrong attitude to elicit a corresponding spirit in a negative re-enforcing cycle. Such downward spirals can be stopped only by someone responding to the releasing power of the Holy Spirit and thereby breaking the vicious circle. God impressed me quite specifically along these lines when our boy was younger than he is now. He had pushed one of his sisters for some minor annoyance which so often assumes gigantic proportions in the eyes of those involved. I reprimanded him rather severely for striking back at his sister in such an ungentlemanly fashion. He flared up and violently informed the whole household that he hated his sisters' irritating ways and wished they were dead! Whereupon I reacted as violently as he had, and the matter developed into a rather superheated situation.

After the smoke cleared away and nothing was left but the ashes of what might have been a wonderful testimony of God's grace, the Lord began to speak to my heart. I was informed that I had reacted to a circumstance rather than responding to His redeeming Spirit. As a father, not only had I failed to lift my son up to a level of greater maturity, but had fallen to his level of immaturity and lost an opportunity for the fruit and gifts of the Spirit to be translated from theory to practice.

The Lord then instructed me as to how I should have responded in firm but gentle wisdom. How much better it would have been to have explained to my boy that there are times when everybody wishes they could get away from it all, especially people! However, life involves people, and we can't always escape from irritating situations. This is the raw material of life which God can use to make us more mature in our responses to unpleasant situations. *In one sense, the family is the testing and proving ground for life as it will be lived in all of its other levels!*

The next time a similar circumstance arose, rather than submitting to a hasty spirit of reaction, I allowed the Holy Spirit to first discipline my own life and then quietly shared the words the Lord had previously given. To our full satisfaction, we saw the Lord actually redeem the explosive situation, not only for our personal insight and edification, but for His own glory and pleasure as well! There is something very gratifying in seeing God perform His Holy Words in the power of the Spirit just when we need it the most.

Another area the Lord loosened up for more of His

life was our time for family devotions. The children had been reared to participate in Bible reading and prayer from the very beginning of their lives. As they approached and entered their teens, I became more legal in enforcing their respect for God's Word and prayer. This, of course, resulted in a reaction to me rather than a response in their hearts to God.

The Lord impressed us that He was more concerned about their hearts being open than some artificial issue about how distracting the presence of the cat might be. Where I used to discourage any discussion other than that which directly pertained to our Scripture reading, now we enjoy a family time that can involve all of the interests or concerns of the day. God's Word and prayer in one sense is supposed to be mixed in with every part of our lives. Too often we make a false distinction between the sacred and the secular, that in effect restricts God to a rather narrow segment of our life experience. *Sometimes we don't realize how spiritually uptight we are until the Holy Spirit sets us free!*

At the time of this writing, we are all still in the process of learning together all that God wants for our home. But we are finding that faith in Jesus and each other is a very satisfying way to live. The Lord is still forcing hidden things to the surface of all our lives for His releasing touch, but He has assured us that His hand of love will never fail, if we purpose to follow Him in faith and obedience. As we have become more restful within our lives, the children have responded in a way which has increasingly brought the joy of the Lord to our home. It is wonderful to really enjoy each other in Jesus!

The principles outlined above have been proven in the homes of many Spirit-filled families across the nation. I know a family in the Midwest who had two wayward children on drugs; yet they stood firm in their faith in God and love for the youngsters. They accepted them back into their home upon their return and steadfastly claimed their full release unto Jesus. God gave them the power and wisdom to go victoriously through some trying days as He worked in hidden, inward ways to reclaim two wayward children to Himself.

God impressed me during the entire time that everything was in spiritual order in the family, even though outwardly the situation was far from ideal. God recognizes hearts of faith and sees as complete that which yet requires time in the natural. Consequently, their home was a source of life in many ways to the Christian community.

They not only maintained a weekly prayer meeting, but were greatly used of God to encourage other parents who, likewise, were going through times of similar distress. How very pleased our Heavenly Father was to see such faith and obedience. The very situation Satan had devised to limit their witness was used by the Lord to display His overcoming and life-releasing power. God really does work everything together for good, and the power of it can be expressed immediately, regardless of outward circumstances. *Jesus Christ is Lord of all—now!*

Many of the references which Jesus made to natural things (little sparrows, lilies of the field, etc.) undoubtedly were first appreciated in a spiritual sense when He was a teenager. The hill country back of Nazareth must have been well known to Him as He communed with His Heavenly Father in the setting of His creation. Jesus never forgot his teenage years, and, in His humanity, has a warm understanding of the peculiar problems of young people. Most faithfully He had obeyed His earthly parents, and thereby learned the discipline which was necessary for His life to find its full and complete purpose.

Respect and obedience are qualities which are as essential for the welfare of society as a whole as at the level of the home. A spirit of rebellion and disrespect in the home which is not corrected in love and wisdom will ultimately produce a person who is sick on the inside. It is a sickness which will infect the world in which the individual lives, an observation which is too obvious perhaps for comfort.

Parental respect is related to the first commandment with a promise—"that it may be well with thee, and thou mayest live long on the earth." The converse is a serious alternative which promises nothing less than death itself—spirit, soul, and body! Sadly, we see in our society today the consequences of God's broken commandment!

The Holy Spirit has come to minister life, not death, and consequently works into our lives the power and desire to honor and obey. There is no way this principle can be violated without forfeiting God's blessing and inviting the inevitable consequences. This is true at every level of family life, both heavenly and earthly. It is necessary to instill this truth into the lives of our children. Even Jesus had to learn the meaning of obedience, or He would have held back from the suffering of the cross. I believe these were lessons He learned initially as a boy in the various demands of family life.

There are Spirit-filled families who so emphasize the permissive side of God's love, they fail to realize there is also a decisive and corrective side as well. *God disciplines those whom He loves!* It is through obedience and discipline that the life principle of the cross is established in young hearts and lives. Sometimes parents can be almost intimidated by the Spirit of this age, which so emphasizes the generation gap that it is assumed any opposition to the desires of our young people will endanger our communication with them. Consequently, parental direction and control is no longer exercised, even though we may discern certain areas of activity as questionable; this tends toward a spiritual deterioration in the home.

Even as this was being written, a phone call arrived from a distressed mother whose son and daughter-in-law are caught up in one of the Oriental cults. At one time both children had been Spirit-filled members of the church. They never learned, however, the discipline of the cross in their lives in their Christian walk. Even when they were children, there was such a permissive atmosphere in the home that their wills were seldom crossed. A part of this involved the kind of music they were allowed to bring into the home against the better judgment and spiritual discernment of their parents.

As has been considered in another chapter, we cannot avoid the cross without opening our lives to the delusion of the Enemy. Even the temptations of Jesus were designed to present the enticing possibility of an earthly kingdom apart from the price of the crucifixion. He refused to disobey His Heavenly Father, however, and firmly confessed His commitment to God's holy purpose for His life. "Thy will, not mine," is still the only way into resurrection life and truth. *Obedience is a sure defense against the deceptive power of the devil.* God requires parents to stand firm concerning the principles of truth which He has designed for the spiritual welfare of the home!

I have endeavored to explain to my own children that I may not always be right in some judgments or decisions, for no one is infallible; yet, I expect them to obey. As parents, we should endeavor to be careful in our demands and quick to admit an error in judgment when we discover it. This might even involve a reversal in decision! Surely this is a grace which the Holy Spirit can give to us in a practical way. Likewise, the Holy Spirit can give to the children the grace to obey even when they may disagree with their parents. In time, if parents and children are united in the Spirit, God can give a common ground of agreement which is pleasing to Him. Where better might we learn to appreciate the harmonizing power of the Spirit than in our homes?

To be filled with the Spirit is to fill our homes with the harmonizing Spirit of Jesus!

90

6

Truth and Error: Principles

The Scriptures clearly indicate that Satan is an exceptionally clever and powerful personality. I once referred to the devil in a public meeting as being a fool. While there was a measure of truth in the statement within the context of the discussion, the Lord later impressed me never to underestimate his power for deception or to imply he was not a foe to be respected. In and of ourselves we will never be able to outwit or overpower our Adversary. His whole intention is to deceive and to destroy and thereby frustrate God's will and purpose for His family. In a most persistent and calculated way he subtly seeks to limit the life of Jesus from finding its full and intended expression in our daily lives.

OPPOSING THE POWER AND PSYCHOLOGY OF SATAN

Satan is a master psychologist — an expert student of human nature — and he clearly recognizes man's potential for evil when divorced from the love and power of God. The story of Job reveals to us that the devil is not omniscient, and his operation against man is in part a matter of maneuvering through an intelligent process of trial and error. He determines the weak areas in our character and corresponding deficiencies in our spiritual armor by approaching our lives in a variety of different ways. He will introduce thoughts into our minds and feelings into our hearts and then carefully watch our reactions. We live in a world which in its character is suffering from the consequences of sin, and we see, even in nature, evidences of disorder, violence, and death. We are not immune from all of the accidents and reverses of everyday life. The Adversary observes our responses to such unavoidable distresses and soon has an accurate measure of our mental and emotional makeup. *Being familiar with our personality profile, he knows what avenues are open for his oppressive and deceptive powers!*

We must honestly recognize the possibility of our being deceived by the devil if we do not rely on God's provisions for overcoming error. I recall reading the passage in Matthew 24:24, which speaks of false prophets endeavoring to "deceive the very elect," and feeling very sorry for all the elect around the world who were being deceived. Then it occurred to me that all the "deceived elect" probably were thinking the very same thing. The genius of deception is that the deceived don't realize it. *In fact, the most efficient deceiver is someone who doesn't know he is deceived himself!* He will be most convincing because no one will detect a note of insincerity in his message.

God has not left His people in a helpless, hopeless state of affairs, however, as if we are nothing more than a Yo-Yo on the end of the devil's string. The Lord impressed me once that I did not have to jump through Satan's hoop every time he placed it in front of me. Actually, God has given us power by His Spirit, when we are rightly related to Him, to not only refuse to jump, but actually wrench the hoop from the hand of the Enemy and wring it around his neck!

The Lord has given to His people power over all the power of the Enemy (Luke 10:19). He also has provided us with both the gifts and principles of discernment that we might detect the Deceiver in his wily ways. Here we see God's Spirit and His truth working together on our behalf to spare us from the devil's subtle snares. We will also come to appreciate the protecting power of the cross of Christ in both opposing and overcoming the Tempter. Here is an interesting story in the Gospels which beautifully illustrates the principles discussed thus far. Let us see God's truth as it is translated into life!

DISCERNMENT THROUGH DISCIPLINE

Peter is an excellent example of a devoted disciple with a heavenly revelation from the Father above. His confession of faith concerning Jesus as the Christ evoked a prompt and warm response on the part of our Lord. Peter the "rock," however, became a "stumbling stone" a few verses further on in our familiar story (Matt. 16:13-24). Here we see the same devoted disciple, completely unaware he had become an instrument of the Enemy, trying to convince Jesus to bypass the seeming tragedy of the cross. *His natural mind and human feelings had become the ground from which Satan endeavored to tempt Jesus to avoid the cross and thereby forfeit the triumph of the resurrection!*

Jesus immediately discerned the source of Peter's dissuasion and moved decisively and emphatically against the devil with a sharp word of rebuke. His personal response to Peter is interesting in that it involves principles which relate to all of our lives when

93

similar situations arise. Peter's deception became an occasion for instruction concerning the truth. Very carefully Jesus explained to him the necessity of the *cross principle* in the experience of every true disciple if the reality of His "life more abundant" was to be forthcoming in his daily walk with God.

It was my privilege to lead a young man and his fiancée into the Baptism in the Holy Spirit one evening in the home of some former students. Both had been involved in the drug scene, and he had recently been released from prison. With their subsequent marriage and his enrollment in the college where I was teaching, a whole new life opened up simultaneously on three fronts — church, school, and home! It was not without the expected adjustments, and God used the problems to present the cross as the only gateway to true resurrection power. *The crown of life can never be achieved apart from the cross of death!* This has very personal and practical meaning which is both basic and essential to the Spirit-controlled life in Christ.

My young friend was an ardent and effective witness for Jesus Christ. His great delight was to share his faith on the beaches of Southern California. He would place his Bible on a mound of sand and soon have an interested and sympathetic audience as he testified about how Christ had changed his life. Many accepted the Lord as their Savior through his personal and persuasive witness. On the homefront and at school the situation was not quite so victorious. Personal adjustments with his new wife were lacking in the fruit of the Spirit. His academic responsibilities were suffering because of the time he was spending at the beach. Lessons were not learned, classes were cut or attended late, and a sense of responsibility was generally lacking.

One day he came by my office to discuss the frustration and confusion of feelings which by this time were becoming somewhat overwhelming. The Lord led us to consider the importance of Christian character and the way it is developed. God has a place of responsibility and a function in life for each one of us in the Christian community. This must be recognized and accepted if we are to be Christ's disciples and mastered by His Spirit. *To be a "disciple" literally means to become a "disciplined one."*

When we willingly submit to the discipline and direction of the Holy Spirit, He gives us the power and desire to "die out" to any diverting or distracting impulses in our lives. Like our Lord, we set our face like a flint toward our "Jerusalem," and without flinching or swerving, joyfully and gladly walk with Him all the way. Not everyone has the privilege of taking up his cross and following Jesus into such resurrection life and power!

In our discussion, God made it very clear that the cross-and-crown life was more than lofty idealism or sentimental thinking. *The Holy Spirit is a very practical Person whose power can bring eternal purpose to every part of our daily lives!* I shared with the young man an interesting lesson we had learned at the home of some Spirit-filled friends. After morning devotions with the family, one of the children announced he was going out to dig weeds from the yard. Another one of the boys added with a laugh that at least they would be working on holy ground. (The entire place had been dedicated to God.) In an unexpected way, the Holy Spirit moved upon one of the young ladies present and she softly responded in a manifestation of tongues. There followed an interpretation informing us that God is indeed as close to us as is the very ground upon which we walk. There is not one step in our daily lives which does not touch the Lord if we love Him and confess we have been called according to His purpose.

Furthermore, the Spirit indicated to us that He takes the earthly circumstances surrounding our lives to bring forth His heavenly purpose through our lives. We were reminded that when God created Adam, it was the dust of this earth which He fashioned and into which He breathed the breath of life.

In other words, God was trying to shape my student friend into the image of Jesus through the very circumstances and responsibilities he was trying to avoid. I explained to him that while student chapel would be a source of inspiration and direction, his home and classroom would be the setting for most of his character building. He then expressed a desire to really become a "disciplined one" and "die out" to his tendency to live life without restraint or responsibility. How fortunate this young man was to learn early in his Christian walk that the cross is the gateway to true personal fulfillment!

SELF-REALIZATION THROUGH SURRENDER

We can really find ourselves only as we first lose ourselves in Jesus! This has some very practical applications in our daily personal affairs. We must be willing to die out to any ambition, desire, or confidence which does not have its origin in God. This includes all thoughts, passions, and imaginations which are not sanctioned by the Holy Spirit. As will be explained later, it often takes the releasing power of the Holy Spirit to *also* yield to the cross our fears, doubts, torments, and depressions! As we do, however, we find ourselves gloriously free in the resurrection life of Jesus!

As simple and obvious as this may seem, many Christians have been deceived by the Enemy into embracing one of two extremes concerning their lives, both of which bypass God's chosen way. Currently there is a rash of books, lectures, and group sessions centered around the theme of self-realization. The emphasis is on knowing, accepting, and expressing oneself. Personal inhibitions are recognized and overcome by honest appraisal coupled with positive thinking, followed by decisive remedial action. The process may even involve prayer and a mixed emphasis on faith in God and self. The cross-life as defined by Jesus is carefully avoided, however.

Now such a program will produce results, but it must be remembered that water rises no higher than its own level. *The self-realization of self has built-in limitations!* Some years ago my wife and I were staying at the home of a Spirit-filled surgeon. In the evening he came home aglow with the joy of a wonderful testimony. A man had come to him for spiritual counsel and confessed his desire to find God for his life. The gentleman had obtained a number of books related to religious science and metaphysics, and with enthusiasm he explained what a change for the better the principles involved had brought to his home and daily life.

At first my surgeon-friend said his heart sank when he learned what a deceptive path the man had taken. But, as he drew upon the Spirit of wisdom and truth, he heard himself say, "That's just fine, and such principles will really work well as far as the things of time are concerned, but apart from Christ, they won't produce a thing that will count for eternity. What you really want is eternal life, which can be found only in the redemptive work of Jesus on the cross!" The man's heart had already been prepared by the Holy Spirit, and he immediately responded by accepting Christ into his life as Lord and Savior. That night he came to the home to be filled with the Holy Spirit, and it was our joy to pray with him.

The Lord impressed me later concerning the

power which is resident in man's mind and soul. Men have built empires and unlocked the mysteries of nature by developing its potential. But at his best, man can never break through the barriers of sin that hold him back from that which is heavenly, eternal, and divinely spiritual. *Apart from the cross of Christ and the power of God's Spirit, man is an earthbound, time-bound, mind-bound and sin-bound creature!* Man has an eternal and spiritual destiny which can never be realized by either his intellect or innate goodness alone. He will never find himself apart from Jesus. Only as he becomes personally acquainted with the Savior can he truly become acquainted with himself. In Christ we see both what we are not, and what we can become. Here is life as it is meant to be lived . . . forever!

The other extreme may also be expressed within a religious guise. It is the deception that the truly noble life is characterized by a self-mortification which almost borders on psychological suicide. Some individuals are plagued with a sense of worthlessness from which they dare not extract themselves lest they commit the mortal sin of self-exaltation. They seemingly are on the horns of a dilemma. Either direction theoretically results in the elimination of their selfhood. Such a position fails to see there is a difference between self-denial and the eradication of personality.

Jesus didn't come to eliminate us as unique identities (as is the objective of many Oriental cults) but rather to set us free to become ourselves in Him! This involves submitting and surrendering our selves to the sovereignty of the Holy Spirit that God's heavenly and eternal purpose *for* us can be fulfilled *through* us — here on earth in time. Again we see the practical and personal side of the Holy Spirit's ministry. As we die out to being centered in self, we find the fountainhead of our being in Christ. He is the integrating theme which relates all the various aspects of our lives most uniquely into God's eternal plan and pleasure! To be self-centered (either in the extreme of realization or mortification) rather than self-surrendered, is to be excluded from the joy of taking up our cross daily and following Jesus into His life more abundant.

It takes the releasing and sanctifying power of the Holy Spirit to transfer the truth of the cross-life into personal experience! Apart from Him, it is impossible to work up even a decent dedication. We are always wondering if our consecration and surrender to God is acceptable. The "law of the Spirit of life in Christ Jesus" lifts us from the heaviness and weakness of such introspection and brings us to the powerful simplicity of the "filled-to-overflowing" life which Christ promised to those who would believe (John 7:37-39; Rom. 8:1-16; Gal. 5:16-25). Again as we shall see, this is most personal and most practical.

SOME PERSONAL TESTIMONIES

Recently my wife and I had the privilege of sharing and praying together with two Roman Catholic sisters during a weekend retreat in the mountains. We were all seated in the restful atmosphere of the surrounding pine trees, which have always been a symbol and source of peace and freedom for me. It was a warm, sunny day softened by the spring breezes which so delightfully sing their way through the trees of the high country.

The lives of these two lovely sisters, however, were far from that which speaks of inner peace and joy. Both were devoted to Jesus and had sought for years to please Him not only by denying themselves many of the usual comforts and freedoms of life, but by deliberately depreciating and suppressing their God-given personalities. Both were rather joyful and

very loving in a natural, outgoing way which demanded expression beyond the limitations they had placed
upon their lives by their religious calling. Years of
frustration and inner conflict had produced both emotional and physical illness. One had required both
psychiatric and medical attention. Both had sought
the Baptism of Jesus in the Holy Spirit, but lingering
questions plus a heavy hold from fears and miscon-
ceptions of the past hindered the full release of the
Spirit through their lives.

We shared with them the understanding that
Spirit-Baptism involves an immersion that is to touch
every area of life experience with the releasing power
of the living Christ. This includes the past as well as
the present. I related an experience God had given to a
lady we had prayed with some years earlier. She had
requested a ministry of deliverance from fear. Her
face was clouded and joyless and she obviously needed
to be released both in spirit and in soul (mentally and
emotionally). Rather than praying immediately, I felt
prompted to share with her the faithful and powerful
ministry of the Holy Spirit which can lift us beyond
our own limitations.

God knows us better than we know ourselves, and
where we might fail in trying to diagnose the source of
our problems, He will not. Furthermore, He is not interested in merely treating symptoms, but in reaching
into the very root of our need, whether it be in our conscious or subconscious life; whether it be in the past,
present, or an imaginary projection for the future. *The
Baptism of Jesus is to touch every part of our life experience!* We then prayed together that the searching
and releasing Spirit of God would meticulously move
through her life from past to present. Every part of the
past was to be reached — people, places, decisions,
mistakes, failures, disappointments, hurts, evil influ-

ences . . . everything! Nothing would be left untouched!

If we saw that at any point an evil force or power had gained access to her life, we immediately confessed not only the dispelling power of God, but the presiding presence of the living Christ. We pictured the Lord opening the drapes and throwing open the windows of her soul that He who is the light of the whole world would become the light of her life. No dark corners or lingering shadows were to remain. The clear, bright, white light of the Lord was to search out every recess and compartment of her being until she became perfectly and gloriously transparent before Him. The fresh, pure breath of God was to revive and restore her staleness of soul and mustiness of mind. The rushing stream of truth was seen as washing through her conscious and subconscious, bringing a healing to her memory. No longer would the thoughts of the past bring pain, torment or condemnation. Jesus was setting her free!

Where past pride, hatred, jealousy, or resentment had found a foothold, we proclaimed the overcoming power of humility, love, compassion, and forgiveness. Personalities involved in the above feelings were released to the grace of God that they, too, might have their lives touched by His. The liberating work of the Holy Spirit once again was setting a child of God free!

So intense was God's power that the woman actually fell to the floor from her chair and joyfully began praising God in other tongues. I assured her startled husband that everything was all right and that God had indeed answered our prayers. She praised God fluently in the Spirit some time before resuming her prayer in English. Whereupon she exclaimed over and over again, "Oh, my Redeemer, my King, my Lord!" She finally climaxed her worship with these beautiful words, "Welcome home, oh, welcome home!" The last

I saw of her, her husband was helping her out the door as she was half-lost in the Spirit. I can still see her hand raised in worship and hear her joyfully confessing that Jesus was indeed her "Lord of lords and King of kings"!

The two sisters with whom we were sharing this story requested that they, too, might experience this inner healing and release for their lives. How very great was their need and desire to really find their freedom in Christ. God had already lifted their faith to a place of holy expectation, so we simply joined our hands and hearts in prayer for each of them. Once again the healing hands of Jesus touched the lives of two of His beloved sisters, as a pine tree and a stone bench became our altar of worship. There was laughter and there were tears, all from hearts overflowing with the joy of the Lord. My wife and I were hugged and blessed profusely and I am sure the angels joined their voices with ours as we sang the song of a soul set free! Subsequent sharing with the two sisters proved the depth and validity of the Spirit's work; the joy and inner release has been lasting.

Perhaps you as the reader have felt your heart burn within you as you have read these words. That is the releasing work of the Holy Spirit bearing witness to the truth. You, too, can be set free this way this very moment. God is no respecter of persons or places. Make your personal prayer and confession. As you do, the mighty rushing river of God's Spirit will set you free . . . now! I can feel the power and authority of His presence as I write, and I know that faith brings the same witness to your own heart and soul. Praise Him profusely for your newfound freedom in Christ. What a joyful confession can be ours now: "If the Son therefore shall make you free, ye shall be free indeed!"

PRINCIPLES OF DISCERNMENT

In traveling about the country and also overseas I became aware that the Enemy has particular patterns of activity designed to deceive God's people and thereby bring limitation, confusion, and division. The apostle Paul exhorts us not to be ignorant of his devices, so let us consider some of the subtle snares which he cunningly employs. We will also see God's answer to deception, which involves both discernment and deliverance. Discernment is based on both spiritual gifts and principles of truth.

Spiritual discernment is a ministry of the Holy Spirit in line with the principles of God's Word whereby we can distinguish between truth and error, light and darkness, life and death, peace and turmoil in the spiritual realm. It is necessary to recognize what is from the heart and mind (affections and understanding) of God, in contrast to that which is derived from the will and pleasure of man and/or Satan. Man can be most persuasive in a strong, soulish way, and the devil can appear as an "angel of light" to the unsuspecting saint. Some situations may convey strong influences from all three sources and present a most confusing picture!

The motivating power behind all of our actions stems from these three centers: God, man, or Satan. The earlier reference to Peter is an excellent example of all three. At one moment he is confessing the Sonship of Christ, and the next he is speaking as "from the mind of men," and becomes the channel through which Satan himself once again tempts Jesus to bypass the cross.

SPIRITUALITY VERSUS SOULISHNESS

A brief discussion concerning the makeup of man

would be meaningful at this point. The Bible sometimes uses the words "soul" and "spirit" synonymously and at other times seems to differentiate between the two. In the distinctive sense, the spirit (pneuma) of man, apart from the ministry of the Holy Spirit, is represented as being lifeless to the heavenly, eternal, and divinely spiritual realm. Man's spirit when quickened by God's Spirit, however, can receive divine revelation and/or illumination; it can respond in prayer, praise, confession, and intercession; it can engage in spiritual witness and warfare and share in the communion of saints; it also becomes the faculty for spiritual discernment.

The soul (psyche) of man may be defined as the seat of personality as it relates to the temporal, earthly, and natural conditions of life. It is the fountainhead of reason, volition, affection, memory, imagination, conscience, and perception of sensory stimuli. Apart from the control of the Holy Spirit, interacting with and through man's spirit, the soulish functions of man cannot apprehend, express, or relate to heavenly purpose. The soul is geared to the spirit of this world and becomes the ground upon which the Enemy of our souls opposes the things of God. Soulish functions, separated from the life and power of God's Holy Spirit, produce character and conduct described in the Scriptures under such terms as: fleshly, carnal, unregenerate, and natural (Rom. 8; I Cor. 2; Gal. 5 TAB).

Man also has a body (soma) by which he relates and interacts with the natural world around him. He senses out the character of his living and nonliving environment and responds either reflexively or reflectively in what is usually a life-promoting fashion. All three aspects of man's being are interrelated and integrated by design into a meaningful whole.

Man lives in a body, but he is more than a body. He has a soul, but he is more than a soul. He is also a spiritual being! When our spirit is alive and submissive to God's Spirit, the soul is inspired to uniquely express the life of Jesus through our physical body to the world without. *In this way, through man, the earthly things of time and nature are related to God's heavenly, spiritual, and eternal purposes!*

No wonder Satan would deceive us into living a limited, two-dimensional, soulish-sensual life apart from God's Spirit. He seeks to disconnect us from our divine destiny and thereby frustrate the will of our Heavenly Father. We are not helpless victims of the devil's deceptive powers, however—Jesus has seen to that! He has sent to us His Holy Spirit, and among His many gifts are those of discernment and deliverance.

We can by God's Spirit discern when the Deceiver is trying to tempt us to "think it through alone" rather than "reasoning together" with God. We will recognize His persistent pressure to focus our faith in our *feelings* rather than the word and life of our Lord. No longer will we view with fear the fantasies Satan paints upon the canvas of our *imaginations.* The paralyzing pain of past *memories* has been healed by the power of God's Holy Spirit. We can actively oppose the Accuser's attempt to strike our *conscience* with the spirit of condemnation. We can joyfully confess that God will work together for good everything that we might *perceive* with alarm or anxiety concerning our natural earthly circumstances. Truly the "law of the Spirit of life in Christ Jesus has set us free. . .!"

With these principles in mind, we will see the Spirit of Truth sharply separating that which is soulish and that which is spiritual in the various problem situations which we shall discuss in the next chapter.

105

We can also further appreciate the meaning of the cross in our daily walk with Christ. As we obediently submit in faith to the perfecting power of the Holy Spirit in our lives, we will simultaneously discover we are "dying out" to soulish powers and pleasures. As we learn to "live in the Spirit," we will become more and more sensitive to that which does or does not produce the life, light, peace, and joy of Jesus! This is the basis of true discernment in Christ.

THE PURPOSE OF DISCERNMENT

We should consider first of all the purpose for which discernment is given. With it comes a great responsibility for us to play a redemptive role in the lives of those about us. The Adversary will oppose our participation in such redemptive efforts by enticing us into the dead-end roads of pride, guilt, or indifference.

The purpose for which the Spirit gives discernment will be frustrated if we allow ourselves to be elevated to a place of pride because we have detected something amiss in a given situation. This can be a particular danger when we share our feeling with others for the purpose of confirmation. There can be a subtle sense of elation that will lay hold of our lives if we are not careful when we discover that someone or a group of individuals have deviated from or fallen short of God's intended purpose in some way. All of us have been tempted along these lines at one time or another and have discovered that genuine discernment can deteriorate into a spirit of criticism coupled with self-exaltation. The grieving Spirit of God can never lay a ministry of intercessory prayer upon a proud person—the redemptive purpose for our discernment will be completely frustrated.

What a paradox is presented when we can seemingly discern everything but pride in our own lives! I know of a man of God who had a remarkable ministry of deliverance which was directed to individuals who had come under demonic influence of one type or another. A false sense of self-confidence developed which subsequently required a ministry of deliverance on his own behalf. How readily we realize that there can be no substitute for the ministry of the cross in our daily lives. *Within its shadow is great safety!*

Pride can obviously destroy God's purpose for discernment but so can a contrasting sense or feeling of guilt. The devil may try to raise doubts and questions concerning our discernment in an endeavor to deceive us. We may be aware in our spirit something is amiss before we recognize what it is at the level of our understanding. In spite of what we sense *within* there may be apparent blessing and success *without.* Much truth and love may even be evident, but yet there is that little red flag of the Spirit which persistently flutters in the periphery of our vision. Others may seem to be oblivious to any signal of danger and joyfully participate in the rising waves of enthusiasm.

At this point we may be tempted to doubt our sensitivity to the Spirit and feel we have fallen heir to an envious, critical, judgmental attitude toward our brothers and sisters. With this comes a paralyzing sense of guilt which renders us useless as far as God's redemptive purpose is concerned. If we try to disclaim our discernment and go along with the situation in a way which implies our endorsement, we find ourselves in a place of great inner conflict and agony of soul. What is God's answer?

First of all, it is always safe to begin at the cross and honestly ask the Lord to reveal to us any soulish shadows of pride, envy, or criticism which may obscure our spiritual vision and confuse our judgment. If after our own lives are cleared, our uneasiness of spirit persists, we should hold fast in faith to our discernment and respond in intercessory prayer. This may be as far as our responsibility goes. On the other hand, God may focus our understanding and require that we move decisively in a ministry of restoration. This will involve the graces of love, patience, and humility, coupled with such gifts as knowledge, wisdom, and faith. These are expressions of the Spirit which will enable us to move with God in a right way, and at the right time with the right people for His redemptive purpose!

GOD'S SPIRIT: A PURIFYING FLAME

It is possible, as mentioned above, to experience situations in which there seems to be a mixture of spiritual blessing and soulish success. One grieves at the violation of spiritual and occasionally ethical principles, yet is confused by the apparent blessing of God in both material and spiritual ways in spite of it all. Great anguish of heart will accompany any endeavor to reconcile in our minds that which cannot be spiritually reconciled!

God brought a measure of understanding to me through His Word concerning such conflicts and later confirmed it one evening by a prophetic word after I had retired. The thirteenth chapter of I Chronicles relates the story of David's desire to return the Ark of God to its rightful place of recognition in the city of Jerusalem. God had ordained the way in which the ark was to be moved from one place to another—it was to be carried by means of poles upon the shoulders of the Levites! The Levitical priesthood represents the spiritual power and authority which is ever the source of divine life for God's people!

David substituted for the priesthood a Philistine

mode of transportation—a new ox-driven cart! In a soulish sense it was a reasonable, rapid method of moving the ark along. The occasion began in a highly successful way. David, God's anointed king, was leading the procession. His motives and purpose were seemingly sincere and straightforward. All the notables and leaders in the entire congregation of Israel were present. There was singing, dancing, and much music. One wonders, however, if some sensitive man of God might not have discerned that all was not as well as the apparent blessing would suggest. Was he perhaps intimidated by the majority who failed to recognize that a right thing was being accomplished in a wrong way? Was he silent when he should have spoken? Or was his voice ignored as one who couldn't relate to the corporate effort?

The cart moved swiftly toward Jerusalem, and our man of God may have wondered if perhaps his judgment had been wrong. Maybe God isn't as particular concerning His principles as had been thought. Then it happened! In one last extreme attempt to stop the procession, God seemingly was prepared to knock the ark to the ground. The oxen stumbled and the ark slid toward the side. A man lifted a fleshly hand to steady the ark and was immediately struck dead by God! (I am sure Uzzah was taken to paradise, but what a tragic way to go.)

It all happened by the threshing floor of Chidon. It was a bitter and painful lesson for David, but a necessary one. If the soulish seeds of doing God's will in man's way had not been uprooted at the very outset, David's temple for a Holy God never would have been built! The spiritual source which provided the wisdom and authority for its erection would long-since have departed. The same is true today. There is a temple of living stones which is rising heavenward, and is to be destined to be an eternal habitation for the Spirit of the Living God (Eph. 2:22). We are those living stones!

Our journey to Jerusalem also passes by the threshing floor. John the Baptist prophetically pictured it in this way: "He [Jesus] will baptize you with fire—and with the Holy Spirit. He will separate chaff from grain, and burn up the chaff with eternal fire and store away the grain" (Luke 3:16-17 TLG). To put it another way, *every stone in God's Holy Temple is going to be fire-polished!*

One night the Lord impressed me in the Spirit that He was going to be moving in an extensive and intensive way in these last days. It is a work which will be done both in and through His people—the Living Church! I questioned if this meant the character-building work of the cross was going to be bypassed, since this involves time and testing. *He assured me no one could avoid the cross and still fulfill his destiny anymore than Jesus could have bypassed the cross and fulfilled His!* I was impressed, however, that God looks at the inclination of our hearts rather than outward appearances, and where He finds wholehearted men who have set their life toward His will, there He intends to do an accelerated work.

Yes, the Holy Spirit will be moving as a purifying flame, reducing to ashes everything in our lives which is soulish in origin, so only that which finds its fountainhead in heaven will remain. This will be true both in a corporate and in an individual sense. This He will accomplish in His way and in His time, but it is as inevitable as the light that accompanies the rising sun. Truly, this is the dawning of a new day—the day of the Lord!

DANGER: POLLUTED WATERS

Only the clean, clear streams of the Spirit are everlasting in quality. There is a spiritual ecology which is as violently opposed to pollution as are the principles of a sound earthly ecology. It is not without purpose that air and water are types of the Holy Spirit. No wonder the prophet Micah warned God's people not to be at ease in the midst of contaminating influences. "Arise and go away: for this is no place for your rest, because the pollution will bring destruction, and the destruction will be grievous" (Mic. 2:10 Lamsa).

The apostle James raises a question concerning fountains that send forth sweet and bitter water at the same time. Such "pollution" ought not so to be! (James 3:10-11). Again we recognize the answer is in the cleansing work of the cross and the sanctifying power of the Spirit which never operate apart from each other. The story of the "bitter waters" of Marah (Exod. 15:23-26), which the Israelites experienced on their way to the Promised Land, seems to refer to those situations in life which force the "bitter roots" hidden within to spring forth in a most evident and obvious way. It took a "tree" provided by God to sweeten the waters at Marah. It likewise takes the "cross" to sweeten and sanctify the fruitful overflow of our daly lives!

The writer of Hebrews correlates these thoughts in these words, "Continue to live in peace with everyone and pursue that purity and holiness of life without which no one will ever see the Lord. Look after each other so that not one of you will fail to find God's best blessings. Watch out that no poisonous root of bitterness springs up among you and thereby contaminates the whole community" (Heb. 12:14-15 various translations). How thankful we can be for the patient, persistent, purifying power of God's Holy Spirit!

To be filled with the Spirit is to know the discerning and delivering power that Christ and His cross can bring to our daily lives!

7

Truth and Error: Problems

With the principles discussed in our last chapter now set in our hearts, let us consider some of the problem areas where Satan's deceptive power is most prevalent.

SOULISH MYSTICISM

On subtle form of soulish behavior is a pseudo-spiritual emphasis that can lead to an unwholesome mysticism. There usually is a great emphasis upon new revelations and spiritual mysteries often accompanied by visions, dreams, and "prophetic" discourses.

Truly, there is hidden truth in God's Word which the Holy Spirit desires to reveal to the diligent seeker. The last days surely will be accompanied by dreams, visions, and prophecy as Peter's Pentecostal message clearly promises. All such manifestations, however, must be tested by God's Word and discerning Spirit. A further and very practical proof of validity is the fruit produced. If a proud, exclusive feeling develops based on secret and superior revelations which only

112

those who have "pressed on" in the Spirit can appreciate, there is danger ahead! Such groups and individuals are inclined to isolate themselves from others, and soon develop a very unteachable spirit.

There will also be a tendency to drift away from the responsibility of sharing Jesus with others as Savior and Baptizer. Such ministry is subconsciously considered elementary and not as satisfying as searching out new mysteries. Home meetings which currently may be very fruitful in reaching the basic spiritual needs of God's children can deteriorate into sterile, inbred fellowships primarily centered around sharing new revelations.

God always wishes to translate truth into life, and there is great safety in allowing the cross to test out our spiritual direction by the fruit it produces in our interpersonal relationships at home, school, work, and the Christian community at large. *We are not really heavenly minded at all if we are so disconnected from this world that we are of no earthly use to God.*

Anything which competes with our daily communion with Jesus and the joy of sharing His life with others can lead to outright error. To become so preoccupied with the supernatural that such manifestations take on a soulish delight can set us up for the lying signs and wonders of the devil (II Thess. 2:9). All supernatural manifestations are not of God. The Deceiver has counterfeits for all of the spiritual gifts. (Suggested reading: Ralph Gasson, *The Challenging Counterfeit*. Logos International, 185 North Avenue, Plainfield, New Jersey 07060.)

So-called spiritual leaders have been seduced into spiritism by approaching the occult from an intellectual (but soulish) point of view. To investigate out of curisoity even the borderline areas of parapsychology apart from God's spiritual defenses is to

113

invite deception and delusion into one's life. It has happened, but needlessly so!

The same could be said for those who out of curiosity submit themselves to the mystery cults of the East. Inherent in these systems is a deceptive power which in the guise of love and truth will darken the souls of those involved. For some, the teachings may appear to be nothing more than interesting Oriental philosophy, but for others they become an open door to demonic forces which require an authoritative ministry of deliverance. No wonder the apostle Paul warned the Corinthian believers lest by any means they be deceived by the subtlety of the Serpent and become corrupted *in their minds* away from the simplicity that is in Christ Jesus (II Cor. 11:3).

PREOCCUPATION WITH SIGNS

There is another natural tendency which can develop as we become warmly aware of God's hand at work in our daily lives; that is, to see or seek to see supernatural signs at every point along our way. *Coincidence may or may not be Providence, and we need to discern the difference!* Biblical numerology is both interesting and profitable, but to read spiritual significance into *every* number which is seen throughout our daily experiences borders on superstition.

The Lord impressed a group of us with His feeling on this matter one evening. We had arrived at a home prayer-and-share meeting after attending a local PTA program. The meeting was under way, and as we discovered later, my wife and I sensed something was not completely in the flow of God's Spirit. Someone had raised a question concerning God's will in a forthcoming decision, and the suggestion had been made that she seek a specific sign of His leading. An element of superstition was subtly mixed into the discussion, and a state of spiritual confusion soon developed.

Suddenly, a lady who had just recently been filled with the Holy Spirit spoke out in a manifestation of tongues. It was like soothing oil upon troubled waters. The interpretation was in the form of an exhortation. The Lord impressed us to be careful in our pursuit of signs lest we become misguided by the false signs of the Enemy. We were cautioned about shifting our faith from God's greatest Sign (Jesus) to that of earthly signs. Our confidence was to rest primarily upon our Good Shepherd rather than on some method of determining God's will. We were assured that the Lord knew just when and where to encourage us with natural signs and would enable us to discern their divine placement. We all recognized the Lord's love and wisdom and accepted His constructive counsel.

The method of setting out "fleeces" to confirm God's will, as Gideon did, seems more of an expression of doubt than faith (Judg. 6:36-40). God had already given His word, but Gideon still wanted two signs he could see before he would believe. Perhaps God in His grace still condescends to our Gideon-like weaknesses at such times of need, but desires a greater expression of faith as we mature. The important principle in guidance is that our faith be fixed primarily in the faithfulness of our Great Shepherd who assures us His sheep will hear His voice. Signs, fleeces, and all other indications then will find their proper place in our lives.

This is not to rule out the possibility that the Spirit may prompt us on occasion to consider a certain possible "turn of events" as a sign from the Lord when our expectation is in faith. *Even here our "sign" will be subjected to the principles of truth revealed in*

God's Word and the inner witness of His discerning Spirit.

There are times when there will be no signs forthcoming at all until we move out in faith and obedience in the direction our heart's desire indicates. The Scripture declares (Ps. 37:4) that if our delight is in being led of God's Spirit, He will give us the desires of our heart. (This can well mean He is substituting our desires for His.) Often God waits for us to explore in faith the "little leading" that we have before revealing more of His will. *What is of God, He will bless by bringing forth the life of Jesus!*

My wife and I, after months of praying for God's will concerning a change, were becoming weary with waiting. The only answer I received was that in the process we were becoming better acquainted with the One upon whom we waited! Finally, the opportunity came most unexpectedly. It involved a major move to the West Coast, and we wanted to be sure it was really of the Lord. All of the necessary practical considerations for moving the family had rather miraculously been provided for. Still we wanted that final witness from God's Word.

The "desire of our heart" was to share the reality of the Spirit-filled life with those who had no "Pentecostal" background. Finally, I discovered this promise in Paul's writings: "For it is God Himself who creates within you both the desire and the power to execute His gracious will" (Phil. 2:13 paraphrase). We made our move on the basis of this, believing if this was not His will and desire, He would let us know. This was the turning point in our lives that led to the experiences that prompted the writing of this book. We could never have anticipated how that desire was going to unfold beyond anything we had ever seen in the past. Praise God, He is a Good Shepherd!

And though the Lord give you the bread of adversity and the water of affliction, yet your teacher will not hide Himself anymore, but your eyes will constantly behold your Teacher. And your ears shall hear a word behind you, saying, This is the way, walk ye in it, when you turn to the right hand and when you turn to the left (Isa. 30:20-21 TAB).

THE LORD IS MY SHEPHERD

One day the Lord impressed me with this question: "Why are you following so many different shepherds?" Upon reflection I realized that whenever I faced a decision or was in a place of spiritual evaluation, I subconsciously was looking more to people than to God. Now there is safety in a multitude of counselors (Prov. 11:14), and the wisdom of mature saints is to be sought and respected; but never should such a privilege become a substitute for counsel with the Good Shepherd Himself. *In the final analysis, God will hold us directly and personally responsible for our walk with Him!*

There is a tendency for us all and especially for the newly Spirit-baptized believer to be greatly impressed by individuals with highly gifted ministries. Such men and women of God are to be truly respected, for they have been placed in the Body of Christ for its profit. Often such saints play a significant role in our relationship with God, and we turn to them readily in our early stages of growth. *There will come a time, however, when the Lord will wean us away from our initial dependency upon people to a more mature relationship of faith in Him.* The weaning process can be painful until we discern what God is doing.

Many times God has placed His "angels of mercy

117

and wisdom" in my path just when I needed them most. I am grateful to the Lord for the gracious gifts of His Spirit which I have received from saintly brothers and sisters. Truly "a word fitly spoken is like apples of gold in pictures of silver" (Prov. 25:11). On other occasions, however, I have sought in a soulish way for God's word of wisdom from some gifted individual who, I presumed, was most qualified to minister to my need — only to be greatly disappointed!

Several times I have been treated almost rudely (not intentionally) by my intended benefactors until I finally realized what God was doing. I remember one godly saint walking off to embrace an old friend just as I was in the middle of an important question which I felt only he could answer. I was left standing alone — with the Lord! In my mind's eye I could see Him looking at me rather knowingly. I responded with a sheepish smile, but didn't say anything. Nothing needed to be said; the lesson was clear!

There will be times when others may become dependent upon us in what may become an unwholesome relationship, spiritually speaking. *True spiritual leadership will lead men to a healthy relationship with Christ which they can share with others rather than a developing dependency upon the leader.*

I recall a foreign student whom I had helped in many ways through prayer and counsel at critical times. It was a pleasure to see him mature into a godly minded young man. After we had decided to make a change of teaching positions, he came by my office to inquire if we were really leaving. He then told me in a touching way that I had been a "spiritual father" to him and how very sorry and discouraged he was to learn that I would no longer be there. I was greatly moved and must admit I shed some tears after he left. Then the Lord reminded me that this was a painful

118

but necessary juncture in his walk with God. Our warm relationship would continue, but in a more wholesome way for the young man. God was making him to become a strong saint who would one day be lending a helping hand to others.

DOMINATING PERSONALITIES

"O Lord our God, other lords beside thee have had dominion over us, but they name alone will we mention" (Isa. 26:13 Lamsa). The Lord has impressed me to be very careful never to depreciate the dignity of personality or to violate the freedom of choice concerning spiritual things which is the privilege of every individual. God honors the sovereignty of man in this sense and will assume control of our lives only by invitation. *The Lord is not a divine dictator who assumes command by force!*

There are spiritual dictators, however, who consciously or unconsciously exert a powerful controlling influence over the lives of others. Some are benevolent in behavior and basic intent and rarely express a strong, soulish spirit unless their position is challenged. Such individuals are often highly gifted in the Spirit and, without fully realizing it in some cases, utilize spiritual manifestations as a means of establishing their authority. *We all have a tendency to elevate charismatic personalities to a place of power and prestige which is good neither for them nor for us.* Many godly people have succumbed to the illusion that they were immune from error because men proclaimed them as infallible. Being deceived themselves, they have deceived others into following their every word without question.

God warned me that His blessing and gifts through our lives could never be a substitute for the

119

work of the cross! This means descending from any man-made pedestals constructed by others. There is an authority and a position which the Lord gives His ministers which needs no embellishment by man. Only that which is grounded in God will survive the shaking which all of us are going to experience as the purifying power of the Holy Spirit loosens us from everything that is unacceptable and displeasing to Him (Heb. 12:27-29).

When I was first baptized into the Holy Spirit and recognized the reality of the spiritual gifts, I was not aware that such manifestations can sometimes have a soulish element which will not minister His life and sometimes not even align with the truth. If anyone indicated God had told them something or added a "thus saith the Lord" to a spoken utterance, I immediately accepted it as the gospel truth! The Scriptures declare we are not to despise or depreciate prophecy, but to test and prove out all things and hold fast to that which is good (I Thess. 5:20-21).

This does not mean we are always probing everything with a suspicious spirit, but rather, continually trusting the Spirit of discernment and truth to alert us to anything not from the Lord. *A prophetic utterance is not be measured in terms of how loud, long, fluent, or flowery it is, but rather how much life, love, and truth it expresses!* I have heard prophecies that have brought much comfort and direction in the Lord and which were most alive with God's Spirit. Others, sadly, were so soulish in origin they ministered nothing but death and confusion.

God holds us responsible for the decisions of life. Never can we allow another, even through a prophetic word, to be the final authority concerning the direction for our lives. Any word which is truly from the Lord will have a confirming witness in our spirit from

'God's Spirit. *Furthermore, it is a witness which will last long enough to be confirmed in other ways!* Some in times past have allowed others to influence their decisions at critical times because they were afraid to question some so-called spiritual revelation or the person or gr up who received it! Consequences in some cases have been tragic.

Many times in teaching and sharing with others (and it applies throughout this book) the Lord has prompted me to instruct the people to accept only what they discern is a ministry from the Spirit. *We are not responsible before the Lord to walk in the light of another person's relationship with God!* We are held accountable only for the light which God gives us and to which His Spirit bears witness. We must learn to trust our Good Shepherd in a direct personal way, or sooner or later we will be led astray in some area by persuasive influences which are not of God. There are times when we need to be delivered from people as much as from the Devil!

My wife went to a meeting where a visiting couple was invited to share. They quickly controlled the time of worship and established a sense of authority and leadership by "prophetic" utterances which were rather harsh and judgmental. The wife of the couple then announced emphatically that God had given her a "ministry of reproof" and she discerned that the group was bound by a spirit of pride. She then declared that God would have them literally humble themselves by kneeling on the floor in repentance. A few of the ladies, who sweetly loved Jesus, were so intimidated by such a strong, soulish presentation, they submitted to the demand in fear and bewilderment. Others were confused, and some left. Here was a situation that required responsible and decisive action firmly based on sound principles of discernment. God in His grace used the incident as a means of instruction for all concerned.

IMPROPER PERSONAL RELATIONSHIPS

There is an important area of deception which must be considered in a rather direct and decisive manner. It involves friendships and other personal relationships which begin innocently enough but develop in an unwholesome way. The common occurrence and similarity of pattern of such problems indicates this is one of the Enemy's ways of insinuating Himself into the very midst of an otherwise beautiful family fellowship in the Lord. The "agape" love relationship between the members of a Christian community is the supreme seal of the Father's approval and blessing. It is not surprising, therefore, that Satan would subtly seek to pervert this relationship.

In his attempt to deprave the holy beauty of Christian friendship, the Deceiver seeks to beguile those involved by appearing as an angel of light. Initially, this is usually in the form of simple rationalization which, if entertained, will become sufficiently elaborate to excuse whatever behavior satisfies their thriving passions. Even relationships which are held short of overt sin can seriously weaken the spiritual life of those involved as well as the community as a whole. Even one-sided "imaginary" affairs indulged in by a single individual can influence others. The Scriptures indicate that where one member of the Body of Christ suffers, all suffer with it. *No Christian lives a life unto himself without influencing others in one way or another.* This is a serious responsibility!

Let us consider some practical aspects of the problems involved. There is a wholesome relationship between the sexes, as brothers and sisters in the Lord, and in some cases, as spiritual mothers or fathers and sons or daughters, which is pleasing to our Heavenly Father. There is expressed in such fellowship a respect and an affection which produces true Christian friendship. There are also the more impersonal teacher-student, counselor-counselee, leader-follower, and even employer-employee relationships within the Christian community which involve necessary interaction between the sexes at various levels.

"It is not good that man should be alone" refers to more than just the intimate relationship of marriage. The experience of man is enhanced by the presence of mothers, sisters, and daughters in the Lord. His life will not be spiritually, psychologically, or socially complete without the ministry of God's handmaidens. The converse is true, of course, for our sisters in Christ. They, likewise, need their spiritual fathers, brothers, and sons to fulfill their lives in God's family. Many beautiful illustrations of this truth are found in Scriptures — including the life of Jesus our Lord!

There is a uniqueness to the marriage relationship, encompassing but surpassing the above, which is ordained of God and should be guarded as most precious. It involves an intimate sharing together in life at every level: spiritually, psychologically (rationally and emotionally), physically, and socially. Marriage has been sanctified as a symbol of the personal relationship of every believer individually, and the Church corporately, with Christ as the Heavenly Bridegroom. It was designed to be the fountainhead of life from which mankind could fulfill the divine call of creation. The sexual function in marriage is elevated to a place of holy beauty and purpose as a unique sign of love and fidelity. No wonder the Deceiver seeks to defile the marriage relationship by extending its exclusive privileges beyond the bounds God Himself has established. In this way the uniqueness of spiritual purpose between partners in marriage is lost!

The Tempter achieves his evil endeavors in most beguiling ways. A Spirit-filled individual may have a mate whose interests are most indifferent or antagonistic to spiritual things. In the course of spiritual fellowship and even Christian witness a genuine affinity may develop for someone who seemingly possesses everything which is so obviously missing in one's partner at home. The relationship may progress no further than a fantasy of the heart and mind. A life is weakened, however, and an estrangement may develop with one's spouse that totally restrains the redeeming power of the Holy Spirit for the home. Such tendencies should be immediately renounced and the releasing power of the Holy Spirit confessed. The Lord cares and understands, but cannot bless a wandering heart. *To persist in such imaginations is to open our minds to outright delusion!*

I know of a lady who actually believed she should leave her husband and marry a man she felt was her true, God-given "soul mate," a man with whom she could "flow together" in the Spirit. This was supposedly even confirmed by "prophecy." She was quite serious about the matter and believed this was the only way "her ministry" could really develop for God's glory. The only difficulty was that her soul mate turned out to be the local rector, who was already happily married with a large family, and quite oblivious of her intentions!

Unfortunately, in some situations, warm overtures of friendship may be welcomed in the wrong way by a lonely and like-minded individual. What begins together as prayer over "mutual problems" can take on a soulish emphasis which is psychologically most overpowering, opening our lives to the deception of the devil. Intimate physical expressions of love and sympathetic understanding may reach an erotic level. If the Holy Spirit's initial warning signals are ignored, the relationship can develop in such a beguiling way that an illicit love affair, for a time, may even seem to be a thing of beauty. *It is not so in God's eyes, and only tragedy and disappointment can be forecast for the future!*

In every case where such situations have fully developed, God has endeavored at many points along the way to bring the discernment of the Spirit. Often this may even be followed by counsel and admonitions from godly leaders of the Christian community. When such warnings are willfully and persistently ignored, the heart and mind can be so deceived that, short of a deliverance, the individual can no longer be reached at all. *Delusion doesn't come overnight; it must be cultivated!*

As soon as any personal relationship develops that is at all questionable, God requires that we take immediate and decisive action. Jesus instructed His disciples along these lines by the illustration of the offending eye or hand. They were to be immediately removed. *We are not to slowly saw our way through, or cut something off inch by inch, but decisively disengage ourselves with one blow!*

I know of a Christian leader who felt a "soul mate" relationship had developed between his secretary and himself. He refused to remove his secretary and give God a chance to reorient his heart and mind concerning his family responsibilities. There is little opportunity for the Holy Spirit to bring clear discernment as long as delusion is being mutually re-enforced by the parties involved.

If the reader feels the Holy Spirit is convicting him about a questionable relationship in his own life, *he should immediately disengage himself from the situation and seek prayer and assistance from a spiritual counselor.* Little light will be forthcoming as long as he remains involved and merely tries to figure it out for himself. "The heart is deceitful above all things" and cannot be trusted after we become intimately and emotionally involved in an unwholesome relationship. We need the detachment which only the Spirit can bring when we in faith have *come apart* and submitted ourselves to His faithful ministry. God is a Good Shepherd!

There is another kind of unhealthy relationship that needs to be recognized. It can develop in a situation where the husband is considered to be less godly minded than the wife. Consequently, she must find her spiritual fellowship and strength from other sources. This may include a special prayer-partner or a ladies' prayer group. Such encouragement is essential and to be greatly appreciated. An atmosphere of love and faith can restore our souls during times of discouragement and despair. I know of a saintly woman who, facing family problems herself, opened her home for wives who wanted to agree together that the Lord would heal their homes. Already God has worked some real miracles in their marriages, and they are united in prayer and purpose that the Holy Spirit will perfect all that He has begun in their midst.

Problems arise, however, where the fellowship or prayer-partner becomes a haven for sympathy and self-pity rather than redemptive prayer and spiritual counsel. This will only foster feelings of hostility and resentment toward one's mate and hinder the healing power God would bring to the home. *Furthermore, there can be an unwholesome transfer of confidence and even love from one's mate to the partner or group.* This need not be in any sexually perverted way, but the consequence is an alienation of affection which will result in spiritual, psychological, and even physical withdrawal from one's marriage partner.

All of this may be accomplished within the framework of something that is supposed to be "spiritual." There may even be mighty manifestations of the Spirit which would seem to confirm this tendency toward alienation, but nevertheless it is an abomination before the Lord. Usually this occurs where there is such an emphasis on "spiritual things" that it implies a withdrawl from such "earthly things" as non-spiritual husbands. This is a false sense of spirituality which is harsh and unlovely. It is in sharp contrast to the faith, hope, and love which characterizes true handmaidens of God.

HALF-TRUTH IS NOT THE WHOLE TRUTH

Many false prophets promote their error by presenting only a part of the truth, carefully avoiding the whole truth. I drove my wife to a ladies' prayer meeting one evening and was invited to remain and share with them. In the course of the meeting they played a religious tape from a weekly series to which they had subscribed.

A deep resonant voice suggested the listener find a comfortable chair and physically relax. One was then encouraged to come away from the cares and pressures of the weary world, and enter into the silence of His presence. Here divine truth and love would clear away confusion and pain and flood one's being with holy light from within.

I opened one eye and saw all the ladies entering

127

into "the rest" as prescribed. The soothing voice of the speaker would have been somewhat conducive to sleep had it not been for a strong sense of inner restlessness in my spirit. The words were peaceful enough, but something was wrong. I prayed that I might not be critical or jealous, but discerning and spiritually alert. After a while it became rather obvious that the divine presence, silence, rest, peace, light, and love of God was at no time centered in Jesus. His name had not been mentioned once!

When the tape was through, I brought this to the attention of the ladies but was quickly and emphatically assured the gentleman was a great man of God through whose life much love and healing had been expressed. With that I pursued my concern no further, rationalizing my uncertain feelings as a personal and cultural reaction to a different approach to spiritual things.

My wife had not responded either, I discovered afterward, and was somewhat disturbed by similar tapes which were played during the weeks that followed. Some of the ladies were seemingly quite mature in the Lord and our first reaction was to depreciate and doubt our discernment.

Some weeks later the gentleman in question was scheduled to speak in the area at a special conference. We were invited to attend and lead a prayer circle afterward. At first I was tempted to decline, but realized this was an opportunity to prove out one way or another the validity of our earlier judgment. The meeting began in a warm and worshipful way and soon was given to the speaker of the evening. He was dressed in the black garb of a monk with sandals on his feet and a tasseled rope about his waist. His speech was forceful, fluent, and most eloquent. Personally, he was most charismatic in character!

The opening prayer confessed that the Father's love was enveloping saint and sinner alike. I felt uneasy about the omission of Jesus as the unique and final expression of that love, but realized that this was perhaps taken for granted. There were references to faith as the way to realize God's truth in our lives, but it was more of a faith in faith than a focus in Christ. There was, however, an occasional reference to our Lord and Savior and I then felt perhaps I had misjudged the man. Other questionable but nondecisive comments were made, and I remained as uncertain as I had been before. A friend of mine had taken a seat next to me, and he seemed to be thoroughly blessed by every word.

As I was holding the entire situation before the Lord, I was impressed to check a reference in the Scriptures I thought I might use in the prayer circle to follow. As I did, I glanced further on in the chapter to read these rather startling words:

> You seem so gullible: you believe whatever anyone tells you even if he is preaching about another Jesus than the one we preach, or a different spirit than the Holy Spirit you received, or shows you a different way to be saved. You swallow it all. . . . God never sent these men at all; they are "phonies" who have fooled you into thinking they are Christ's apostles. Yet I am not surprised! Satan can change himself into an angel of light. (II Cor. 11:4, 13-14 TLB)

Then an unexpected thing happened. I saw a vision of a shining golden pole or shaft. Encircled around it, but not in actual contact with it, was a slender, bright green serpent. It wasn't an ugly viper, but more like a graceful grass snake which is not only

129

harmless but rather charming in appearance. (Some foreign snakes of this description are extremely deadly.) I recall raising the question in my mind, "What in the world does this mean?" Immediately there was an almost audible reply: *"Ever approaching, but never touching the truth!"*

The kind of Jesus that Paul preached is our standard of Truth. Born of a virgin, the Son of God becomes the Son of man. He was the express image of God; He uniquely died for our sins and arose in resurrection power. He ascended to the right hand of the Father, from whence He sent forth the Holy Spirit. He will come again, as He left, to judge both the living and the dead and thereby determine their destiny for heaven or hell. This is the Jesus that Paul preached! This was not the Jesus that was presented by the ministry in question.

This answered my questions, but the final confirmation came months later when some of the literature of his ministry came into my hands. I discarded the materials into the wastebasket, but felt impressed of God to retrieve it for purposes of examination. There in bold print was a denial of the unique power of Christ's shed blood for the remission of sins. Sin was not viewed as man's self-willed way in rebellion to God, but rather an error in thought which did not appreciate man's innate goodness. Salvation was defined as recognizing the truth concerning the divine flame of light and life within each man which awaits to be expressed as we submit to the royal law of love.

No need for the redemptive work of the cross; man can be his own savior. If he fails to realize the truth here, he will experience it in heaven where God's life and love will be fully expressed. Judgment is experienced now and is the result of a life lived in error. There is, therefore, no need to prepare for a day of divine reckoning, and most certainly there is no place for hell in God's great heart of love.

Such a thesis is most appealing to the natural mind. *But, what a cruel fool it makes of our Heavenly Father for allowing His Son to die on the cross after He pleaded to be spared if there was any other possible way for man to be redeemed.* What a mockery of God's grace! Such is the error that prevails when another Jesus other than Paul's Jesus is preached. When Jesus declared He was *the* way, *the* truth and *the* life, He really meant that He was the *only* way, the *whole* truth, and life *everlasting.* Truly, there is no other way to the Father! Paul's Jesus is indeed a powerful standard against which we can measure truth and error.

THE MYSTERY OF BABYLON

And upon her forehead was a name written, Mystery, Babylon The Great, The Mother Of Harlots and Abominations of The Earth. (Rev. 17:5)

The word "Babylon" means "confusion" and historically refers to the confusion of tongues which came because of the erection of the Tower of Babel. The tower symbolizes man's arrogant attempt to "reach into the heavens" by his own efforts. It was designed by man, built by human hands, and totally earthy in its composition. While most appealing to the natural eye, it was an abomination to the Lord, for every brick was befouled by the sweat and smell of soulish endeavor. *Here was man's attempt to unify and dignify himself apart from God's purpose and power!* Instead of blessing, however, it brought a divine curse and confusion. So it is today wherever men substitute their soulish systems for the life, power, and divine order which only the Blessed Holy Spirit can produce.

Such earthly towers of men stand out in clear

131

contrast to the beautiful Temple of God which is arising unassisted by human hands (Acts 7:48; Eph. 2:19-22). We are the living stones of His workmanship finding our place in His Temple by divine appointment (I Pet. 2:4-5). *All other constructions produce only pride, suspicion, and division among the members of the Father's family!* The spirit of Babylon always produces a strong sectarian attitude in the lives of those possessed and thereby inflicts wounds within the Body of Christ. No wonder the Scriptures exhort God's people to "Come out of her . . . that ye be not partakers of her sins, and that ye receive not of her plagues" (Rev. 18:4).

Basically and initially, "coming out of Babylon" is an inner change of heart which shifts one's loyalty from an earthly framework, with its man-made fences, to the true vision of the Church which the Holy Spirit is universally revealing to those who have been Spirit-baptized by Jesus Christ. Real charismatic communities become fountainheads of resurrection life for the dead, dry bones of Christendom long since buried in the sterile traditions of men (Ezek. 37:1-14). Perhaps this is one of the "greater works" Jesus promised we would do after He ascended to the Father! (John 14:12).

Some equate all "organized churches" as synonymous with "Babylon." That the spirit of Babylon is manifested in some denominational systems is not to be denied. It is also found, however, in "non-denominational" fellowships and even in informal church-in-the-home groups. *It is one thing to take "people out of Babylon" and another thing to take "Babylon out of the people"!* Many local groups have succeeded only in building their own little towers related to doctrine, patterns of worship, and governmental control. Each considers itself to be the true expression of "the local New Testament Church" and often will recognize no other assembly as really "legitimate." Such an exclusive attitude is denying the very basis for true fellowship in Jesus.

One is impressed with the apostle Paul's exhortation concerning division in the Body of Christ as expressed in I Corinthians 1:10-17. The Corinthians were basing their fellowship around men. Paul indicates that all were in error, even those who boasted they were of Christ, because of their exclusive attitude. No one would recognize the other, and division was the result.

There are some subtle forms of deception which are related to this kind of division. *The groups involved usually emphasize obedience to those in positions of local authority above the responsibility of the individual to the Lordship of Jesus personally!* As a result, homes and families have been split, and a legal, loveless attitude develops. The strong dominating power of such groups may be hidden until a difference of opinion concerning spiritual things is raised. Great emphasis is placed on personal submission to the ruling elders or "Body" as a whole. This is enforced by intimidation. To disobey is to invoke God's wrath! Because there is much apparent blessing and truth in many respects, one can fearfully question the discernment the Spirit of truth is actually revealing to them. I have counseled with many confused and frightened people who have been hurt and scarred by such misguided ministries. It is beautiful to see Jesus heal and set them free!

The Holy Spirit is going to be shaking, sifting, all of Christendom at every level in these days before us. This includes our own lives and Christian communities as well as others who we have always felt should be shaken. (We would even help the Lord out when it comes to the others!) At the same time, we are going to be surprised to see God's Spirit moving in places

133

which perhaps many of us thought were out of bounds. The Holy Spirit readily moves into some of the "strangest places" to reach searching souls and hungry hearts!

Sometimes the Lord leads individuals out of their local situations; other times He leaves them in as "missionaries" to their own people. The demoniac of Gadara, after his deliverance, requested that he might leave the area which had been so unreceptive to Jesus and follow Him as a disciple. The Lord wisely refused, but rather told him to go home to his people and share the goodness and love of God with them. He obeyed and was able to present a witness in an area that wouldn't have accepted Christ in person! (Luke 5:1-20). *We may not be able to change "the establishment," but we can bring the life and love of Jesus to those whom God has prepared us to serve!*

Furthermore, if one's church is truly Christ-centered and Bible-oriented, there is a stability and safety which such fellowship can afford as one matures in his newfound walk in the Spirit. There is much to learn from all of our brothers and sisters, even those who may not presently understand the charismatic renewal in the churches. Many of them have moved further out into the stream of the Spirit in some areas than we have fully realized. In some situations, we need them as much as they need us in God's overall view. We must ever guard against pride and be as humble and honest as we know how in the Lord.

Not every pastor in the "organized church" is an example of the "blind leading the blind." Many accept their responsibility as under-shepherds with utmost sincerity and are concerned for the immature and even obstinate sheep within the fold. *Love is patient and long-suffering, as Jesus was with His disciples!* Even Judas was treated with understanding until his decision against the Lord was finalized and

134

he separated himself from the fellowship of the disciples. Wherever possible, may we bring blessing rather than confusion and division.

The seeds of love and truth grow quietly but most irresistibly if God has prepared the soil. The "gifts" must be set in the "graces"! The gifts were designed to be clothed in the fruit of the Spirit to be fully effective in God's glorious purpose for His people. The best testing and proving ground for God's work in our lives is often the very setting in which we were placed when we met Jesus Christ as the Baptizer. Some of the finest and most beautiful fruit of the Spirit is grown in just that kind of soil. A hasty spirit has probably limited God's witness more times and in more ways than we realize. I know my wife and I have always felt we were premature in resigning so soon from our local church following our blessing in the fullness of God's Holy Spirit. We never really gave the Lord the time He needed in expressing to others our Blessed Baptizer. Perhaps others can profit from our mistake. *We are responsible for discerning not only God's will and His way, but also His timing!*

Babylon represents the soulish schemes of man which substitute worldly traditions for the direction and power of the Holy Spirit, and it is also the fountainhead for outright Satanic delusion and deception. As mentioned before, he will often appear as an angel of light within a "spiritual" or even "religious" context. The Scriptures clearly define and emphatically renounce all such devilish deceptions:

> Keep to your spells then and all your sorceries, for which you have worn yourself out since your youth. Do you think they will help you? Do you think they will make anyone nervous? You have spent weary hours with your many advisers. Let them come forward now and save you, these

135

who analyse the heavens, who study the stars and announce month by month what will happen to you next.

Oh, they will be like wisps of straw and the fire will burn them. They will not save their lives from the power of the flame. No embers these, for baking, no fireside to sit by. This is what your wizards will be for you, those men for whom you have worn yourself out since your youth. They will all go off, each his own way, powerless to save you. (Isa. 47:12-15 JB)

When you come into the land which the Lord your God gives you, you shall not learn to follow the abominable practices of these nations. There shall not be found among you any one who makes his son or daughter pass through the fire, or who uses divination, or is a soothsayer, or an augur, or a sorcerer, or a charmer, or a medium, or a wizard, or a necromancer.

For all who do these things are an abomination to the Lord; and it is because of these abominable practices that the Lord your God is driving them out from before you. You shall be blameless (and absolutely true) to the Lord your God. For these nations, whom you shall dispossess, listen to soothsayers and diviners, but as for you, the Lord your God has not allowed you to do so. (Deut. 18:9-14 TAB)

Other related passages include: Exod. 22:18; Lev. 19:26, 31; 20:6, 27; Deut. 4:19; 13:1-5, 17:2-5; II Kings 9:22; 17:16-17; 21:2-6; 23:24; I Chron. 10:13-14; Isa. 8:19; 47:9, 12-14; Jer. 8:1-2; 14:14; 19:13;27:9-10; 29:8-9; Zeph. 1:4-6; Acts 16:16-18; 19:19; Gal. 3:1-3; 4:10-11; 5:19-21; Rev. 9:20-21; 18:23; 21:8; 22:14-15.

Sorcery refers to the practice of the occult arts under the power of evil spirits. In modern language, such practices include: fortune-telling, palm reading, card reading, Ouija board, seances, spiritism, development of extrasensory powers (ESP), hypnotism, spirit writing, water witching, psychometry, black and white magic, astrology, yoga, and other mystic cults. To personally and directly explore any of these areas even out of curiosity can lead to serious Satanic oppression. Not everyone with such experiences in his background has been so influenced, but many have, as the author can confirm from personal counseling experience.

The Scriptures repeatedly denounce and warn against involvement in any form with the above activities, as harmless as some of them may seem on the surface. (There is a rash of parlor games designed to test one's extrasensory powers.) In the Old Testament economy, violators were sometimes stoned, so serious were such offenses before the Lord (Lev. 20:6, 27). In the New Testament we are clearly informed that all sorcerers (practitioners of the occult) will find their part in the lake of fire (Rev. 21:8).

Even Spirit-baptized Christians have been deceived into pursuing one area or another without realizing the related danger. Astrology can be presented in a beguiling way as a spiritual blessing which has been ordained of God to enhance man's welfare. *This is a lie, and to willfully submit to what God has cursed will lead ultimately to spiritual darkness and delusion!*

Perhaps the reader has not been aware of the seriousness involved in such activities up to this point. The Lord stands ready to forgive and release you from the influence of such relationships in the past. *God requires only a deliberate renouncement of all such activity on your part and a confession of Christ's releasing power!* He is the Lord of our lives, and as our Good Shepherd, He assures us of His protection and guidance both now and for these important days before us.

DEMONISM

There are those who scoff at the reality of Satan as a personal intelligence with a host of evil spirits (demons) to assist him in his opposition to God's will here on earth. *There are so many references to the devil and his demons in the Bible that to deny their existence would be to deny the personality of Christ and the holy angels, if we wanted to be logically consistent.* Obviously Satan would not have us take his kingdom seriously in any personal sense since this would lead to real Christians taking up their armor and engaging him in spiritual conflict (Eph. 6:10-18).

Many relegate demonic activity only to Bible history and deny the influence of demons in modern times. Others believe their power is experienced only in primitive cultures as evidenced by stories from missionaries. With the rapid increase of evil in our own country, however, more are ready to believe something is behind perversion and atrocity. Still, some may not realize that demonic oppression of Spirit-baptized saints is possible, and blame everything but the real enemy for their affliction. Obviously, relief is forthcoming. *God is restoring a sound, wholesome ministry of deliverance to the Body of Christ.* He wants His people free to move forth in the full force and power of His Holy Spirit. There is nothing more beautiful than to see individual lives not only being released from the hold of the Enemy, but then ministering deliverance to others who have been bound by Satan's power.

Not every problem in life is demonic in origin. Satan in his cunning way would deceive us into embracing error by starting with the truth and then taking us beyond its limit. If we cannot be misled into denying or ignoring demonic power, the devil will entice us into becoming preoccupied with it. *Some people spend more time confessing demons then they do the Lord!* They assign every adverse circumstance to demonic activity. Every weakness of the flesh, in themselves and others, is viewed as the direct result of demonic influence. As a result, they become fearful and suspicious and unknowingly cast a spiritual shadow upon all whom they encounter. The Enemy revels in such attention and praise.

Others, instead of becoming fearful, develop a very proud and critical spirit as they analyze every problem and every person in terms of demonic power. They become self-styled "deliverers" who, by virtue of their strong personalities, intimidate more sensitive individuals who submit to their ministries out of fear. I heard of one person who was "turned over to the tormentors" because he refused to "cooperate" in a prayer for deliverance. The story was finally shared with the person's Spirit-filled pastor who immediately released the individual in Jesus' name from her fear and anxiety. Such episodes cast shadows on genuine ministries of deliverance which are usually very balanced in their character.

The true test of a wholesome, balanced ministry is the "life" that is forthcoming in the Christian community as a whole after it leaves! If division, confusion, and uncertainty are the results, something is out of divine order. This does not mean there may not be some blessing and even many supernatural manifestations of the Spirit, but the real test is still the healing life of Jesus for His entire Body.

As mentioned before, true deliverance involves spiritually discerning the problem both in terms of *source* and the *method* or means God would choose to bring a release. We live in a sin-cursed world and are subjected to the downward pull of our soulish natures apart from the Holy Spirit. The disorder, ugliness, pain, and death which is a part of our natural world is Satanic in origin but not necessarily demonic in expression. There are not thistle-and-thorn demons or hurricane demons, but both are manifestations of a creation which waiteth for its redemption (Rom. 8:19-23).

This is not to deny the possibility of direct, demonic activity involving natural phenomena in some cases. I have always felt the storms on the sea of Galilee which threatened the life of our Lord and His disciples may have been more than just meteorological disturbances. Generally speaking, however, most natural distresses can hardly be designated as demonic in origin. Nor is the Christian immune from all such natural disorders. *Where not protected, however, we are perfected, for God will work all things together for the good purpose of conforming us into His image! (Rom. 8:28-29).*

Likewise, the works of the flesh are expressions of our carnal natures and not always direct evidences of demonic activity (Gal. 5:19-21). To knowingly and persistently yield to such weaknesses of the flesh or to indulge in excesses of anything which weakens us spiritually or physically is, however, an open invitation in some cases to demonic influence. *What begins under our control leads us into a subjection which is overpowering!* In such situations, only the power of Jesus can set the person free.

Some people, in blaming demons for everything, fail to see they are avoiding their responsibility to face themselves before the Lord. It is easier to obtain "instant holiness" through an exorcism than it is to submit daily to the sanctifying power of the Holy Spirit that we might take up our cross and follow Jesus. *The prayer-chair of deliverance can never substitute for the day-by-day ministry of the cross in our lives!*

Where genuine demonic influence is limiting a life, God wants to express His love by releasing that life completely to His Son. Some individuals are so bound they may have almost lost their will to the power of the Enemy. God can set them free by the prayer of faith and the authority of Jesus' name. *Such a release, however, can be maintained only if they choose to remain free!* Some individuals enjoy communion with spirits that feed on their fleshly appetites. Some enjoy the attention or pity which their condition evokes from others and don't really want to be free.

I prayed twice for a lady who put on a spectacular dramatic display of demonic power and control. The first time, I sensed a desire for show and attention and after prayer warned her never again to give in to this soulish desire for recognition. She was actually attracting and feeding demon powers which were most willing to gratify her desires. The second time she tried the same thing, I was unaware it was the same person. She was writhing around on the floor, and the whole Bible class was rebuking all kinds of spirits as she identified them. This went on for some time, until I finally recognized who she was.

I dismissed the class, except for a few ladies, and sharply told her to get up and conduct herself in a seemly fashion. She obeyed with some reluctance, and I could discern the Deceiver was trying to bluff his way out of the situation. I explained we would be pleased to decisively pray for her full release if she would repent of her desire to yield to the spirit of self-attention. *The next step was not prayer, but repentance!* She stubbornly refused. The Spirit had pierced through her phony display and revealed the intent of her heart, but she would not repent of her sin. She didn't want to be delivered. She thoroughly enjoyed her "deliverance sessions."

Many times God requires a person to cooperate in his own release. I shared for some time one afternoon with a student who was really bound spiritually and psychologically when she first arrived. As we shared together around the Lord, God's truth was progressively setting her free, and she became more relaxed. Finally, only one chain remained, and this related to her willingness to submit to the Spirit of praise, which at one time had beautifully graced her life. Instead of sovereignly releasing her from the heavy hold of the Enemy in this area, God gave her the key and required she unlock the chain herself as an expression of faith and obedience. She did, after some wavering between the voice of God and that of the Devil, and she immediately found the freedom she sought.

A young woman who was tormented by timidity which limited her spiritual ministry in song requested prayer for deliverance. But instead of prayer, it was suggested she resist the Enemy herself in the name of Jesus. Demon powers can be weakened by refusing to give them the attention they thrive upon. They feed upon our fears and self-directed thoughts. Our power to resist and overcome increases as we feed upon God's truth and give attention to His Son by much praise and worship. Our faith becomes strong by praying and actively sharing His life and love with others. She was wisely encouraged to minister from time to time, and finally she found joy in actually offering to sing for God's glory. She progressively found real liberty and power in her ministry for the Lord.

The principles involved were clearly confirmed by a vision she received from the Lord. She saw what had been a great, black gorilla chained in her backyard. The creature was dead; nothing remained but a mass of hide and bones. The once powerful creature had been *starved* to death!

The Lord is revealing to His people the various ways by which the Holy Spirit can bring release to those who are oppressed by the Enemy. *Many have been set free by the power of God's Word alone!* I recall sharing in a Bible class the account of the lady referred to earlier in this chapter who was bound by fear but released as we prayed the Holy Spirit would move through her past life in healing power. All at once a lady in the audience began to laugh in an almost uncontrollable way. She had just been gloriously set free herself as she had listened in faith to this story of God's liberating power. This has happened many times through the ministry of the Word without any formal prayer being offered. I have claimed that many who are reading this chapter will experience God's liberating power in their own lives by confessing their own deliverance. Often only two people are really required for such an experience — you and the Lord!

Sometimes in Spiritual Life classes we have analyzed the cause and consequences of fear which Satan would exploit in our lives. The first time I shared along these lines, the Lord brought a change in presentation I hadn't planned on. God prompted the class to share their fears and the fruit such fears produced. People shared things never before admitted, only to find others were plagued in the same way. It was interesting to see the common patterns that the Devil uses in oppressing God's people. *Often he deceives us into thinking nobody else has our kind of fears!* If we believe our problem is unique, we will question if we can really be helped. For instance, usually over sixty percent of each class questioned has felt at one time or another they had crossed God's line of grace by committing the unpardonable sin! (Incidentally, if one had so grieved the Holy Spirit, his conscience would be so seared he would have no concern whatsoever about spiritual things, including his eternal destiny.)

Here are some of the objects of fear which Satan would magnify into dark clouds of oppression: death, sickness (as cancer), failure, criticism, rejection, ridicule, future, war, mental breakdown, old age, financial distress, accidents, natural catastrophes, loneliness, responsibility, unpardonable sin, second coming of Jesus, eternal judgment, decision, missing God's will, witnessing, praying aloud, and the phobias (dark, high places, people, crowds, water, animals, etc.). Do any of them sound familiar?

The following consequences of fear are listed, as they too were presented by class members: depression, discouragement, anxiety, confusion, frustration, tension, weakness, self-pity, melancholy, introversion, self-depreciation, bitterness, anger, isolation, procrastination, indecision, irrational behavior, etc. No wonder the Scriptures declare "fear has torment" (I John 4:18).

The Son of God has been manifested that He might destroy these works of the devil (I John 3:8). "The thief cometh not, but for to steal, and to kill, and to destroy: I am come that they might have life, and that they might have it more abundantly" (John 10:10). The Scriptures declare that we can overcome the Adversary because, "Greater is he that is in you than he that is in the world" (I John 4:4). This same indwelling Christ has assured us that He has given us power to tread on serpents and scorpions (demon powers), and over all the power of the Enemy: and nothing shall by any means hurt us! (Luke 10:19). If we first submit to God's Son, God's Spirit, and God's Word, we can resist the devil and he will flee from us

(James 4:7). *You can overcome Satan now by the blood of the Lamb and the word of your testimony!* (Rev. 12:11).

Each oppressed person is a different situation, and the discernment of the Lord is necessary to determine God's chosen way of release. *To rely upon a given method or formula is to invite disappointment and confusion!* Sometimes the Lord will supernaturally reveal the root of the problem which has given the Enemy his power over a life. It may be an attitude (resentment), a wound inflicted in early life (a specific incident), or a suppressed feeling of guilt that God wants brought to a place of conscious recognition in the light of His healing power.

Sometimes it is necessary for the person to share at length as the Spirit clears his life through the healing of his own spoken word before the Lord. At other times, such sharing gives the listener spiritual insight into both the basic problem and God's answer. Many surface problems are only symptoms of, or even smoke screens for, the basic need. On some occasions, what is needed is the ministry of God's Word followed by intercessory prayer.

In other situations, discussion would be utterly fruitless, and only a decisive prayer for deliverance can open the mind darkened by delusion. A direct command to the demonic spirit to leave in Jesus' name can bring immediate relief. Stubborn cases may involve prayer and fasting and the ministry of several agreeing over a period of some time. More than one session may be required. I have seen God work in stages in some lives that had been deeply involved with evil powers. Deliverance may or may not be accompanied by physical manifestations (coughing, spitting, convulsions, or vocal outbursts). It is not wise to encourage such responses, but one can quickly explain should such things occur and questions arise.

At this point in my experience, I think discretion should be used in presenting the message of deliverance with the intention of mass exorcism. People can be brought psychologically to a place of fear which is not the conviction of the Holy Spirit at all and leads to confusion and unnecessary distress. To encourage coughing and spitting during the process can also create an opportunity for the Enemy to magnify his presence. *There is a fine line between the power of suggestion, which is of man, and the power of conviction, which is of God!*

I have heard people confess to being delivered from the spirit of pride when I had the uneasy feeling they had been coerced by psychologically induced fear to request deliverance from a demon when the real answer was the work of the cross! A girl once almost glibly requested I pray for her "deliverance," as she was familiar with this ministry of exorcising demons. I didn't sense anything of a spiritual nature such as this and should not have even prayed. I did pray a general prayer for her release to Jesus, and she immediately responded dutifully by coughing and announced she felt much better. The whole thing was psychological!

I have on many occasions, however, sensed a real spiritual power was oppressing one of God's saints, and a sharp command in the name of Jesus brought an immediate release from tension, depression, pain, etc., followed by joy and relief. One lady with suicidal tendencies did respond by coughing, but most have not. *I have the feeling that if the Enemy cannot keep God's people from a genuine deliverance ministry, he will endeavor to exploit it in a way which exaggerates his power and leaves confusion, fear, and a preoccupation with demons!* This is often followed by a rash of self-styled deliverance ministries which actually exalt the devil more than the Lordship of our Christ.

This has been of genuine concern to me, for deliverance is a ministry which is desperately needed in the Body of Christ. *The casting out of demons is as much a ministry of the church as is salvation and healing!* (Mark 16:15-20). It certainly characterized the apostolic age and needs a wholesome and proper emphasis for our day. Satan is moving with great power and wrath, for "he knoweth he hath but a short time" (Rev. 12:12). This ministry will become increasingly important as the evil of our hour increases. It is apparent on every hand!

CONCLUSION

Let us pray that God will give His wisdom that the Enemy cannot pervert God's purpose in setting His people free. *The Devil's tactics have always been to so depreciate God's gifts in the hands of man, through misuse and abuse, that they will be brought to total disuse!* This has been true in all of the manifestations of God's Spirit which are evident expressions of His power: tongues, healings, miracles, etc. May we be bold for God, but in a wise and understanding way, that His full purpose in all of the gifts of the Spirit will be forthcoming.

May we also reaffirm God's desire that through His Spirit we may truly learn to be ourselves in Christ Jesus and thereby freely express His life to others. The Lord Himself releases us from the errors of the past and beckons us to arise and come away with Him. *God wants us to know we are free to follow His Son, for we will never respond to a freedom we don't believe we have!*

I was interested in the newspaper account of the African animals that were shipped to the West Coast recently to populate a newly developed wildlife entertainment center. When the cages were opened, some of the animals bounded out into the freedom of their new home without hesitation. Others remained within the confines of their little cramped cages and actually had to be prodded out into the open fields. Both groups of animals were released when the doors of the cages were opened. Only one group accepted their freedom and responded accordingly. The other group had been so conditioned by their long confinement they could not accept the freedom they were intended to have. They likewise responded accordingly!

The Song of Solomon (2:8-13) beautifully pictures for the Christian the invitation of our Beloved Bridegroom to experience the freedom in life which only His Spirit can bring to our longing hearts.

> The voice of my beloved! behold, he cometh leaping upon the mountains, skipping upon the hills.
>
> My beloved is like a roe or a young hart: behold he standeth behind our wall, he looketh forth at the windows, shewing himself through the lattice.
>
> My beloved spake, and said unto me, Rise up, my love, my fair one, and come away. For lo, the winter is past, the rain is over and gone;
>
> The flowers appear on the earth; the time of the singing of birds is come, and the voice of the turtle is heard in our land;
>
> The fig tree putteth forth her green figs, and the vines with the tender grape give a good smell. Arise, my love, my fair one, and come away.

To be filled with the Spirit is to be filled with the Truth that sets and keeps us free!

148

8

Trials, Testing, and Temptation

When Jesus too had been baptized and was praying, the Holy Spirit descended upon Him in a visible form like a dove, and a voice came from heaven, which said, You are my much loved Son in whom I am well pleased. . . . And Jesus being full of the Holy Spirit returned from Jordan and was led by the Spirit into the wilderness where He was tempted for forty days by the devil. (Luke 3:21-22; 4:1-2 various translations)

Here is an account in the life of the Spirit-filled Christ which deserves the study of every Spirit-filled Christian. How often we have heard someone remark, "I thought this walk in the Spirit was going to be a path of peace and joy; I have had nothing but trouble since I surrendered my life to Jesus as my Baptizer I don't understand what is happening!" Not everyone is plunged immediately into problems following their Baptism in the Holy Spirit, but some are, and all of us will experience trials and temptations at one time or another if we purpose to be totally led by God's Holy Spirit.

149

Satan is a hard loser, and we can't really expect him to obligingly pat us on the head for acknowledging the Lordship of Christ and thereby challenging his claim as the god (champion) of this world. He is actually hoping to knock us completely out of the ring of life by getting us to pull our punches through fear or ignorance. Fortunately we have the best Trainer in the game. He knows firsthand every strategy which our Adversary might endeavor to use against us. His counter-strategy is perfect, and we can be a winner every time — just as He was. However, we had better learn well the rules of the game!

There are spiritual laws and principles in the contest between good and evil which God would have us know and apply. *Sometimes we are subjected to unnecessary or unduly prolonged distress because we fail to effectively oppose the Enemy as we have been instructed to do.* How easy it is to get depressed and discouraged during a time of testing and then be tempted to give up and "throw in the towel." We are assured, however, that if we *first* submit to God — His Son, His Spirit, His Word — we *then* can effectively resist our Adversary, and he will turn and run away in defeat (James 4:7). There is an important priority in action here which we dare not overlook! May we learn, therefore, how to translate principles into practice and live victoriously for God's glory. He wants us to win very much!

PRACTICAL INSIGHTS FROM THE PSALMS

The Psalmist was personally aware that life's pathway is not always flooded with sunlight. The twenty-third Psalm presents this truth by a very vivid study in contrast. The opening verses describe our Good Shepherd as leading us beside the green grass and still waters of a lovely meadow.

Upon the canvas of our imagination, there develops a beautiful pastoral scene. Soft spring breezes chase fleecy white clouds across an azure sky. We picture ourselves resting in the warmth of the sun's golden light as lazy insects buzz from one fragrant flower to another. The colorful scene is completed by the happy sounds of the songbirds as they harmonize with the lilting laughter of a nearby brook. The merry little stream soon broadens and deepens into the still, quiet beauty of a lovely reflecting pool. Surely this is the joy, rest, and peace which are promised to the Spirit-filled Christian!

The day's journey, however, is not yet complete, and the Good Shepherd now arises and moves intently on with quickened pace. It is with some reluctance that we follow along, wondering what could be so important as to take us away from the green grass and refreshing waters of our mountain meadow.

The trail gradually narrows and descends ever more sharply as we go. Shadows are closing in upon us now, for the setting sun is lost behind towering pinnacles of naked rock. It is noticeably colder, and the chilled air amplifies the strange sounds of the night which seem to be closing in from every side. Soon everything will be enveloped in a darkness so deep no sign of the path or the Shepherd will be seen. *It is difficult to even remember what a meadow is like when one is in a shadowed valley!*

Strange thoughts can cross one's mind while we are passing through the valley. Does my Good Shepherd know where I am? Does He care about my condition? Have I been forsaken and forgotten? My great desire was to follow Him, or I would never have left the meadow! Why, oh why, did this happen to me? Jesus, are You there? Are You there?

151

How encouraging to hear His voice in reply. "Do not be afraid, for I AM with you. I will not leave you nor forsake you. Your night is as the day to me. You cannot see me, but I can see you. I will comfort you with the rod and staff of my guidance and protection. Furthermore, there is a special banquet and anointing which is to be found only in the valley. Some of the finest fruit and greatest gifts of My Spirit are perfected in the valley of trial and temptation. Don't doubt, but follow Me in love and obedience for there is divine purpose in the direction we have taken together."

The following words from the Psalmist further reenforce our confidence concerning the care of our Great Shepherd during times when we might be tempted to doubt or give way to despair in the darkness.

O Lord, you have examined my heart and know everything about me. You know when I sit or stand. When far away you know my every thought. You chart the path ahead of me, and tell me where to stop and rest! Every moment, you know where I am. You know what I am going to say before I even say it. You both precede and follow me, and place your hand of blessing on my head.

This is too glorious, too wonderful to believe! I can *never* be lost to your Spirit! I can never get away from my God! If I go up to heaven, you are there; if I go down to the place of the dead, you are there. If I ride the morning winds to the farthest oceans, even there your hand will guide me, your strength will support me. If I try to hide in the darkness, the night becomes light around me. For even darkness cannot hide from God; to you the night shines as bright as day. Darkness and light are both alike to you. (Ps. 139:1-12 TLB)

The Lord is encouraging us never to doubt in the dark what we have learned in the light!

FOR GOODNESS' SAKE

There is indeed a heavenly purpose which can be realized in our lives during times of trial and testing. The Scriptures do not promise that everything that happens to us is good — but that all things can work together for good! (Rom. 8:28). We must understand how God defines "goodness," or we may miss His purpose entirely. What is the yardstick by which He will measure the "good and faithful servant"? (Matt. 25:21).

The first use of the word "good" in Scripture is found in the Genesis record of creation. God Himself is speaking and proclaims His creation as good — as very good! Good for what? A few verses later we are startled to hear Him say something is not good. "It is not good for man to dwell alone." Why is it not good for man to dwell alone? What is His measure of goodness? The answer is a personal one. God's measure of goodness is a man — a perfect man — and, that man is Jesus Christ! *God's only begotten Son was the model into whose image man had been created.* The Father's desire has always been to have a family of many sons whose lives were to be fashioned after that of their Elder Brother. This obviously is the answer to our question concerning the kind of "goodness" toward which "all things" work if we really love God and accept our calling in His divine purpose. There is absolutely nothing that can happen to us that He cannot use to make us more like Jesus and thereby prepare us for our particular place in the family of God. Our Heavenly Father is concerned with building the character of His Son into the lives of His children!

Very often we have memorized the familiar Scripture of Romans 8:28, mentioned above, but have missed the message which completes the passage in the twenty-ninth verse. Let us listen again with fresh understanding to the divine answer from Paul's pen concerning all of the trying things that thread their way into the tapestry of our lives:

> Now we know all things continually work together for good to those who love God and are called according to His plan and purpose. For from the very beginning, God decided that those who came to Him — and all along He knew who would — should share the likeness of His Son, that He might be the Elder and Model Brother in a great family of many sons. (various translations)

This passage is truly encouraging when we realize the "all things" which God will work together for good include our faults, failures, mistakes, and deficiencies as well as our talents and achievements, if we surrender them to the redeeming power of His Holy Spirit!

I can never re-live my past college days, which were pretty much wasted as far as any real witness for Christ was concerned. Yet God in His redeeming grace has allowed me the privilege of working with college students most of my professional life. It is easier to be patient with others when they are trying to find themselves when we realize how long-suffering God has been with us. Doubts, fears, impulsive efforts for self-

154

recognition are familiar landmarks on the well-beaten path of personal experience.

Many servants of the Lord have shared a similar testimony with me. The Holy Spirit is likewise redeeming their past through the lives of others who have listened to their counsel and profited thereby. We don't all have to make the same mistakes in the same way. There is no such thing as a life so completely wasted that God cannot redeem it in some way for His glory!

TRIED FOR A TWOFOLD PURPOSE

There is a twofold purpose for trials and temptations: the *proving* and *perfecting* of our character. Weaknesses and deficiencies are forced to the surface where they can be faced without fear, for we are assured of God's redeeming grace. Even repeated failures during times of testing teach us how much we need a power beyond ourselves if we are going to overcome. God has given us that power in His Holy Spirit!

God will never condemn us for our failures, but will use the occasion for our correction and instruction. A good example is Peter's walk on the water following the Lord's invitation to step forth. He did well and almost reached Jesus when the severity of the storm caused him to doubt and sink in despair. With eyes filled with fear, he looked back to the Lord and cried out, "Lord, save me!"

I am so glad for what Jesus did not do. He could have looked at Peter in disgust and pointing a finger of condemnation, shouted, "Run out of faith on Me will you, Peter? All right for you; you deserve a watery grave, and I am going to stand by and watch you go under!" The thought of such a response is ridiculous — we know the story so well. I wonder, however, if in the midst of our own stormy seas, Satan does not try sometimes to deceive us into thinking that God has turned His back on us in our moment of failure!

How Jesus did respond is both encouraging and informative. Two things happened. First, he immediately stretched out His hand and caught Peter. (The Lord is always in touching distance.) Then He taught him more perfectly the way of faith. He *caught* him and He *taught* him! He catches us and He teaches us in like fashion. *Victory is born out of failure when that failure is touched by the hand of God!*

The proving-perfecting process prepared Peter for another walk of faith. One year later, Peter would stride out in faith upon a sea of humanity that could have taken him to his death as it had his Lord some forty days earlier. But Peter's stand was strong, and his voice was powerful as he preached his Pentecostal sermon. What might have ended in tragedy turned out to be the glorious birthday of the New Testament Church — the first charismatic community! Peter had learned his lesson, but it is well to remember his classroom had been a stormy sea!

It is with an authority based on experience that the apostle Peter writes these words concerning the necessity for fiery trials:

> Because you have put your faith in God, you are under the protection of His power as you wait for the salvation which is ready to be revealed at the end of time. This means tremendous joy to you, I know, even though at present you are temporarily harassed by all kinds of trials and temptations. This is no accident — it happens to prove your faith as fire purifies gold which ultimately will perish with this world. Fire-tested faith has an abiding quality which is far more precious to God than perishable gold! This proving of your faith is planned to result in praise and honor and glory in

the day when Jesus Christ is revealed (I Pet. 1: 5-
7 various translations).

APOSTOLIC COUNSEL FOR
MODERN-DAY DISCIPLES

All of the apostles were men who wrote and ministered from the realm of reality. They were not ivory-
towered theorists, but battle-tested and scarred soldiers of the cross. Their words carry the weight of
truth which has been translated into life, and even
proven by the price of death. According to tradition,
all of the apostles except John gave their lives for the
faith. Although separated in time, they are our brothers in Christ, and their counsel is inspired by the Lord
to encourage us to stay steady in our faith during
times of trial and tribulation. They knew whereof they
spoke!

I was quite moved to learn that the apostle James
senses the same family feeling of love and concern for
others as did his earthly and heavenly brother, the
Lord Jesus. (Traditional scholarship assumes James
to be the brother of Jesus.) Some sixteen times James
addresses his readers as "brethren." There is a warm
but authoritative tone which characterizes his letter.
"What a noble man speaks in this Epistle! Deep unbroken patience in suffering! Greatness in poverty!
Joy in sorrow! Simplicity, sincerity, direct confidence
in prayer!" (F.W. Farrar *The Early Days of Christianity*, p. 324).

As brothers and sisters with the same high calling
in Christ, let us listen to what our brother James
wants to share with us.

When all kinds of trials and temptations
crowd into your lives, my brothers, don't resent
them as intruders, but welcome them as friends!
Realize that they come to test your faith and to

157

produce in you the quality of endurance. But let the process go on until that endurance is fully developed, and you will find you have become men of mature character with the right sort of independence.

And if, in the process, any of you does not know how to meet any particular problem he has only to ask God — Who gives generously to all men without making them feel foolish or guilty — and he may be quite sure that the necessary wisdom will be given him. But he must ask in sincere faith without secret doubts as to whether he really wants God's help or not. The man who trusts God, but with inward reservations, is like a wave of the sea, carried forward by the wind one moment and driven back the next. That sort of man cannot hope to receive anything from the Lord, and the life of a man of divided loyalty will reveal instability at every turn.

The man who patiently endures the temptations and trials that come to him is the truly happy man. For once his testing is complete he will receive the crown of life which the Lord has promised to all who love him (James 1:2-8, 12 Phillips).

The apostle Paul is another proven pioneer of the faith who knows what it is to plow through rocky ground (II Cor. 11:23-30). Hear his voice of experience:

But remember this — the wrong desires that come into your life aren't anything new and different. Many others have faced exactly the same problems before you. And . . . you can trust God to keep temptation from becoming so strong that you can't stand up against it, for he has promised this and will do what he says. He will show you how to escape temptation's power so that you can bear up patiently against it. (I Cor. 10:13 TLB)

It is apparent from Holy Scriptures that what God will not protect us from, He will perfect us through! Trials and temptations have the twofold purpose of testing and toughening our character. They also provide the opportunity for really getting acquainted with Jesus and ourselves as well!

THE SOUL: THE SOIL FOR TEMPTATION

We could define a *testing* as adversity in *outward* circumstances to which we can respond in the Spirit or react in the flesh. *Temptation*, then, might be considered as *inner* inducement to sin in thought, word, or deed (James 1:14-15). Obviously the concepts overlap, for we can be tempted to evil during our testings, and our characters are being tested during temptation (James 1:12).

The inner ground of our being which provides the soil for temptation is the soul. As mentioned earlier, it is the seat of our personality and the source of such soulish functions as reason (thinking), volition (willing), affection (feeling), memory (recalling), imagination (creating), conscience (discerning), perception (interpreting sensory stimuli). All such activities, you recall, are to be subservient and under the control of the Holy Spirit. When uncontrolled by the Spirit, they become the tools of temptation by which Satan can limit God's power and purpose in and through our lives.

The Devil will tempt us to elevate our intellect and reason to the throne of our lives. In a proud, independent way we will become the "Master of our fate" and the "Captain of our soul." The tree of knowledge is still growing in the garden of our lives, and it always brings an exalted sense of soulish pleasure to sit beneath its shade and eat of its fruit. The scepter of decision resides in our hands — we shall determine what is right and wrong, good and evil, for our own course in life! The ultimate result? Strong-minded, self-willed individuals who are walking in the darkness of delusion thinking they are in the light!

Sadly, the prevalent philosophy of education often cultivates this kind of intellectualism. Truth is not centered in the meaning which Christ can bring to our existence, but rather in the individual himself. *The Lord Jesus alone is the integrating theme and key to life — but only as His Lordship is acknowledged!* No wonder we can't put ourselves together, let alone the world!

Others are tempted to allow their passions to rule their thoughts, conversation, and conduct. Their consuming desire is for a steady diet of sensual and worldly pleasure. Such self-gratification leads to a very little life, that is never large enough to lovingly embrace others or the Lord. The hole in their lives is really a bottomless pit which even eternity cannot fill! In the other extreme, the Enemy would tempt some to doubt God's love and goodness for their lives, and continually torment them with painful memories, fearful imaginations, and a condemning conscience. Usually when on this topic, I have asked audiences to indicate how many have felt they had at one time or another crossed God's line of grace — going beyond the point of forgiveness. Inevitably, two-thirds to three-fourths of the people respond affirmatively!

THE TEMPTER'S QUESTIONABLE TACTICS

As we grow in Christ and become grounded in the faith, the Tempter will approach our lives in more subtle ways. This we can understand in a rather revealing way by using the five journalistic questions — why, how, when, who, where — as an approach to his tactics.

(why). When we can readily discern between what is right and wrong, we may be tempted to do a right thing for a wrong motive. I remember my first chapel presentation as a faculty member of a well-known Christian university. During my time of prayer and preparation, I told the Lord with some feeling that I would really appreciate it if He would help me to make a good impression, since the occasion was obviously rather important.

The Lord's reply was short and direct: "Why do you want to do that?" As I turned the thought over a few times, I began to realize how mixed our motives can be sometimes. Of course we want to glorify God and be a blessing to others, and sincerely so, but along with it, maybe we want a little polish for the old "image." There is a fine line between wanting to be our best for God, and being our best in the eyes of man.

Ever since Adam and Eve were tempted to become like gods apart from God, men have sought to establish their dignity and destiny by their own efforts. The Tower of Babel is an outward endeavor which expresses an inner attitude.

Come, let us build us a city, and a tower whose top reaches into the sky; and let us make a name for ourselves. . . . Their inward thought is, that their houses will continue for ever . . . ; they call their lands their own . . . and after their own names (Gen. 11:4; Ps. 49:11 TAB).

How easy it is for all of us to move from mixed motives and seek to establish our own name and project our own image under the guise of promoting "our ministry." We can be so easily deceived by the Tempter when it comes to this area of our lives. The Lord impressed me once that in one sense it wasn't "my ministry," but "His ministry through me" for which I was personally responsible before Him!

(how). Even doing the right thing for proper motives can be spoiled if the Enemy can tempt us to do it the wrong way. It is the old story that "the end justifies the means." Actually, improper means will ultimately destroy the end! The previous reference to King David's attempt to return the ark to Jerusalem on a new cart is an excellent example (chapter 6, the section entitled, "God's Spirit: a Purifying Flame"). Peter's ear-severing sword-swing is another illustration (Matt. 26:50-53). Our warfare is not against flesh and blood, but against principalities and powers and wickedness in high places. The battle we are fighting is on the spiritual level! (Eph. 6:12). The very weapons we use are not those of human warfare but those powerful in God's warfare for the destruction of the Enemy's stronghold (II Cor. 10:3-4 TLB).

Above all take on the great shield of faith . . . the sword of the Spirit which is the word of God, and pray always and in all ways in the power of the Holy Spirit! (Eph. 6:16-18 various translations).

Peter had failed to pray as the Lord had repeatedly encouraged him to do while they were in the Garden of Gethsemane. When the soldiers and religious rulers

162

arrived to take Jesus, Peter, relying upon human passion and reason, attacked a human foe with a human weapon and lost a spiritual victory! He failed the test, but through it he learned a lesson about spiritual warfare. He shares it with us in his first epistle.

> The Lord is watching his children, listening to their prayers; but the Lord's face is hard against those who do evil. . . . If you will humble yourselves under the mighty hand of God, in his good time he will lift you up. Let him have all your worries and cares, for he is always thinking about you and watching everything that concerns you.
> Be careful — watch out for attacks from Satan, your great enemy. He prowls around like a hungry, roaring lion, looking for some victim to tear apart. Stand firm when he attacks. Trust the Lord; and remember that other Christians all around the world are going through these sufferings too (I Pet. 3:12; 5:5-9 TLB).

Not only is our warfare to employ spiritual weapons, but our witness to the world is to be characterized by spiritual purity. If the Devil can't keep us from wanting to witness, he will endeavor to dilute our efforts by the use of worldly ways. We can never gain heavenly ends by employing soulish means. Our desire to "communicate" can lead to compromise. The Holy Spirit is not bound to past programs of evangelism, which desperately need re-evaluation, but He cannot honor methods which violate God's principles.

It is true that people have to be reached at their level of interest and need, but how easy it can become to rely more on modern methods of entertainment than on the attracting power of the spiritual gifts. The latter can be expressed in many ways, including through the Fine and Performing Arts, but in an attitude of humility before God which keeps one totally dependent upon the Holy Spirit.

Mixing worldly methods with spiritual endeavor is sowing "soulish" seeds into the lives of new converts, which ultimately will produce a harvest of weeds. The fine fruit we had hoped would abide can be completely choked out. We will reap what we sow. The Tempter knows this law of the spirit only too well and subtly uses it to his own advantage!

(when). Right things done for right motives and in right ways can also miss the mark if accomplished at the wrong time. God's perfect will involves His perfect timing. It is a hard thing to be disqualified from the race for repeatedly "jumping the gun." There have been several times when my wife and I (mostly me!) have undergone unnecessary distress because we wanted to hurry up a decision before God was ready for us to make it. How I have complained because the Lord wasn't providing the direction I felt a Good Shepherd should when I, as His eager sheep, wanted to go racing out into the dark alone.

We once had a jumpy, black and white neurotic cat to which we gave the rather inappropriate name of "Tex." We took Tex with us to the bay in Galveston for a few days of vacation one summer. I decided to put a little red harness on the cat and attach him to the clothesline. When he was released, we witnessed a rather remarkable performance. The cat took off like a skyrocket, and coming to the end of his line he was promptly jerked high into the air. Upon his descent, he took off in the other direction for another dramatic flight into the blue. It took some time to settle him down.

It might have been a little bit funny, except that it reminded me somewhat painfully of some of my

164

own "fast starts" for God. How thankful we can be for the "harness of the Lord" by which we can learn His timing. Most of the time the Lord is not in the hurry we are. Andrew Murray's little book, *Waiting on God*, is a must for those who really wish as disciples to walk in step with their Good Shepherd.

(where and who). God's will not only involves right motives, means, purposes and timing, but also proper places and people. Oftentimes the wrong places can involve us with wrong people, and wrong people can take us to wrong places!

Where do we go and to whom do we turn in our time of need? Do we seek counsel and prayer with those who are wise in the Lord in the Body of Christ, or do we turn immediately to men of the world because our problems have some "practical" aspects to them which require "professional" attention? God can use "men of the world" in the solution of our problems, but they cannot minister to the spiritual center of our need. This, however, is where the answer has to begin! The practical outworking then is from within to without, but under the protection and direction of the Lord which was established in prayer with other members in the family of God.

The Scriptures inform us that there is great safety in a multitude of counselors (Prov. 11:14). The Christian community was ordained of God as a place of healing, help, and counsel for His people. We need each other in the Lord. No wonder Satan is always trying to disconnect us from the wisdom and assistance which can only be found in the Body of Christ. This is His chosen place, and these are His chosen people!

The study of temptation as it revolves around the questions outlined above could be greatly expanded. Perhaps this approach has provided a framework which can be further developed by the reader in a practical way as the Holy Spirit faithfully applies the principles involved. Our desire now is to see how some of the insights concerning trials, testings, and temptation can be enhanced even more by studying the life of Jesus. The Scriptures emphatically state that He was tempted in every respect as are we, yet without sin. For this reason He is a High Priest who can sympathize with us during our times of trial and testing and to whom we can turn for help in our hour of need (Heb. 4:15-16).

THE TEMPTATIONS OF
A CARPENTER'S SON

The temptations of Jesus as the Son of man (God cannot be tempted) can be considered in three phases: pre-baptism temptations, forty-day wilderness temptations, and post-wilderness temptations. Prior to His baptism by John in the Jordan River, Jesus underwent some thirty years of rather commonplace living as far as the world was concerned. He was looked upon simply as the carpenter's son.

It is of some significance to realize that the eternal wisdom of the Godhead chose a carpenter shop in the little village of Nazareth as the training ground for His development. It was here He grew in stature, wisdom, and favor with both God and man (Luke 2:52). It takes time and testing to mature. Jesus matured spiritually, intellectually, emotionally, physically, and socially. *He was tempted and tried in all areas of His life, for upon His shoulders was going to rest the full weight of man's redemption!*

I suppose we all wish there were more details concerning the "silent" years of His life. Apparently they were so ordinary, in contrast to the three years of His

166

active ministry, little was considered significant enough for the Gospel historians to record! I have always felt that many of the illustrations He used from nature and ordinary life were rooted in the experiences of His boyhood and young manhood. (Rosemary Houghton's book, *The Carpenter's Son,* is a biographical novel for young and old that is historically and scripturally accurate. There is a spiritual quality to her writing which readily moves into the heart of the reader.)

The home, the shop, the synagogue, the marketplace, the wooded hills, the occasional trips to Jerusalem were all a part of His youth. Each situation provided opportunities to meet humanity in all of its diversity of expression. Wherever people are there are problems and temptations. Jesus learned well what was in the heart and mind of man.

It took time for God's Eternal Son to mature into perfect manhood. How differently some of us would have planned His life. We would have sent Him out as a boy evangelist at the age of twelve and added some eighteen precious years to His earthly ministry! Our Heavenly Father chose to do otherwise, however, so Jesus spent thirty years in the carpenter shop and three years in the ministry. *Not one year or one moment was wasted, however, for God's timing is not only perfect, but filled with purpose!*

I don't think everything Jesus did in the carpenter shop was perfect, but I think he stayed with it under Joseph's careful supervision until it was! I am sure Joseph never gave him tasks beyond His ability, but suited each responsibility to the appropriate level of His apprenticeship. Jesus learned the hard way, just as you and I do! I am sure there were broken blisters and cut fingers and aching muscles. Perhaps He was even tempted on a particularly tiring day to

167

leave some promised work unfinished that He might escape to the hillside to rest and pray. He never did! He learned to establish priorities and faithfully fulfill His daily responsibilities.

A friend of ours once had a vision of Jesus during the days of His early manhood. Joseph had already died, and Jesus had assumed the responsibility of supporting the family by His carpentry. He was well qualified for His trade by years of hard work. He knew how to select the proper tree to supply the wood for a given task. He took professional pride in His workmanship, for His was a labor of love. He was very diligent in His carpentry, which involved long hours of hard labor each day. His arms were strong, and his hands were calloused. In the night hours, He spent much time in communion with His Heavenly Father.

She saw Him on the last day He spent in the carpenter shop before leaving for His earthly ministry. He carefully brushed the sawdust from his final piece of work, which seemed to be some kind of a bench or table. Rubbing His hand over the smooth wood, He looked satisfied that His task was now complete! Folding His carpenter's apron and setting His tools in their proper place, He moved decisively to the door, where He lingered briefly a moment for one last look about the carpenter shop. Then He stepped across the threshold and firmly closed the door without a backward glance. Our friend was caused to know that He was on His way to the Jordan River to meet John!

INITIATION INTO THE EXTRAORDINARY

Jesus had faced all the trials and temptations of ordinary life, but now He was about to begin a most extraordinary ministry. The description of His baptism by John in the Gospels is significant in the details which were selected for the reader (Matt. 3:13-17; Mark 1:6-11; Luke 3:16-22; John 1:23-34). Jesus submitted to water baptism by John, not because He needed to repent, but to "fulfill all righteousness." The latter relates to acknowledging and obeying all that has been appointed of God. *It was a public act of submission to God and identification with sinful man!*

This is amazing to think about. John preached that the kingdom of heaven was at hand; that the way of the Lord must be made ready; that a mighty Baptizer in the Holy Spirit was soon to come. Then standing before him was the King — the Lord — the Baptizer! What words of power and authority would He speak? What mighty works of wonder would He perform? Initial impressions are so important!

His very first act was one of submission; His very first words were those of prayer, for as He came up out of the waters of baptism He was praying (Matt. 3:16; Luke 3:21). At one time I wondered what Jesus might have been praying about on such a significant occasion. I was frankly disappointed His prayer had not been recorded. Now I am not so sure we have been left without any indication whatsoever. His entire life was one of submission to His Heavenly Father. One can almost hear His words: "My Father which are in heaven, hallowed by Thy name. Thy Kingdom come? Thy will be done on earth as it is in heaven. . . . Truly not My will, but Thine be done!"

Then it happened! The Father, looking upon His submissive Son, fulfilling all they had planned together in eternity past, could restrain Himself no longer. The heavens were opened — and with great feeling and authority He spoke. "Thou art my beloved Son in whom I am well pleased!"

The Spirit Himself likewise bore witness, descending upon Him like a dove. Jesus obediently assumed the authority and power which the responsibility of Sonship required. The mantle of God's Spirit rested upon His life as He prepared to *proclaim* the Word of God and *perform* the works of God to a world waiting to hear and see. The apostle John emphasized the spiritual authority of His ministry in these words: "For this one — sent by God — speaks God's words, for God's Spirit is upon him without measure or limit" (John 3:34 TLB).

Jesus was about to move under the power and control of the Spirit into a new order of life. With it He was going to face temptations of a force and quality hitherto unknown. New levels of authority and responsibility will always be challenged by Satan in a corresponding way. Jesus was no exception — nor are we! Let us see what lessons we can learn from the temptations of the Spirit-filled Christ.

To be filled with the Spirit is to be filled with the same overcoming power which controlled the life of Jesus!

9

The Temptations of the Spirit-Filled Christ

Then Jesus full of the Holy Spirit returned from Jordan, and was immediately led by the Spirit into the wilderness with the wild beasts. There He fasted and was tempted for forty days by the devil. (Matt. 4:1-2; Mark 1:12-13, Luke 4:1-2 synthesized account)

The number forty appears many times in Holy Scripture. It usually is associated with a time of trial, testing (proving out), and temptation, sometimes involving tribulation and judgment. There were forty days of rain during the Noachian flood (Gen. 7:4); Moses was forty years on the back side of the desert (Exod. 3:1); (Acts 7:30); Moses was forty days on Mount Sinai receiving the Law (Exod. 24:18); Moses was forty days praying and fasting that God not destroy his people (Deut. 9:25-26); the spies were in the Promised Land forty days (Num. 13:25); the Israelites wandered for forty years in the wilderness (Heb. 3:15-17); Goliath harassed the Israelites for forty days (I

Sam. 17:16); Elijah traveled forty days in the wilderness on the strength of "angel food" (I Kings 19:8); Nineveh was given forty days to repent (Jon. 3:4).

Moses represents the law, and Elijah, the prophets. Both fasted forty days during times of stress and travail. Jesus, the fulfillment of the law and the prophets, underwent His time of intense testing and temptation as well and on similar ground.

PLANT A GARDEN IN YOUR DESERT

The first Adam was tempted in the midst of a garden paradise. Failure drove him from that garden into a world that was to share in the curse of his sin. Therefore, it was onto the cursed ground of a desert wilderness that the Second Adam was driven for His time of temptation for *God desires His sinless Son to be the first of many sons who following the example of their Redeemer will reclaim their spiritual heritage on the very ground from which it was lost!*

For forty days, Jesus experienced the harshness of His surroundings without shelter. It was horribly hot during the day and cruelly cold at night. The ground was dry with little vegetation save the thistles and thorny cacti characteristic of the desert. Jackals, hyenas, wolves, vultures, serpents, and scorpions were His only companions. How very different from the garden paradise of Eden. Jesus was not spared the consequences of man's sin as it involved the whole realm of nature. Yes, it was into the desert He was sent!

As with Jesus, we, too, are not immune from the pain, disease, disorder, catastrophes, and accidents of life which are a result of a sinful man living in a creation cursed by his fall. While God in His grace has retained some of the original beauty and harmony of His

172

once perfect creation, ugliness, discord, and fatal imbalances are readily evident as well. Neither the physical nor the living world was spared. Tornadoes, hurricanes, earthquakes, drought, floods, and fatal freezes all speak of a disequilibrium in nature. The cry of the predator's victim, pestilence, famine, disease, and finally death are evidences of imbalance and discord in the living world as well.

Not all of our afflictions are directly due to Satanic attack or demonic influence, although ultimately he is responsible. This is not to say God cannot use such disturbances for His own purposes on occasion, as in the case of Job's family (Job 1). On the other hand, if we sit on a thistle and get stuck, we can hardly blame a "sticker" demon. Likewise, it is rather misleading to refer to devastating storms and earthquakes as "acts of God." Many of our misfortunes and accidents are purely a result of living in a world disordered by the curse of man's original sin.

God does place a hedge about us in many ways, but what He does not *protect* us from, He will *deliver* us out of, or *perfect* us through. He can indeed work *all things* together for good. We will be a winner in any case. *In other words, let the Lord plant a garden in your desert!*

I was approached by a lady one evening following a meeting where the speaker had placed great emphasis upon faith for physical healing. A number of miracles had occurred, and there was occasion for much praise and great rejoicing. There was no praise in the heart of this daughter of God, however, nor joy upon her face. Her face and hands had been severely scarred by accidental burning a year or two earlier. Frustration and resentment now filled her life, as one healing meeting after another had left this wife and mother without help, healing, or hope.

Many times she had been the object of people's prayers, and eventually, repeated failures had filled her heart with bitterness. Well-meaning friends had blamed her lack of faith for her failure to be healed, and now she was in the depths of despair. Why had this happened to her? Why were others healed and she was not? Had God lifted His hand and hidden His face from her life in her time of exteme need? Painful questions, indeed! Were there any answers? Was there any hope? Oh, why, why, why?

As I held her crippled hands in mine, I felt there was much God was wanting to say to her, for spiritual scars are vastly more significant and serious than physical scars. It was important for her to see that her accident was not an "affliction" *from* God's hand, but a natural tragedy which could become a "triumph" if placed *in* His hands. The Enemy is quick to take advantage of our ordinary misfortunes and utilize them as avenues by which he can invade our lives with doubt, fear, and frustration. *As with Job of old, he would tempt us to "curse God and die" or even worse, "blame God and live in bitterness."*

The Lord, however, is full of compassion and concern, and wills to begin His healing work within our hearts. Spiritual healing produces a purity of life that will last forever. Furthermore, it brings us to a place in God's purpose where we can appropriate healing at other levels of our need when God's time is right. Meanwhile, there is a special ministry of both praise and service which is most pleasing to the Lord. With these thoughts in mind, I encouraged my afflicted sister in the Lord to "cast not away her confidence" concerning God's love for her, but to return it to Him in unceasing prayer and worship. She then could have the unique joy of sharing that love with others who, like herself, might be walking a lonely path and look-

174

ing for someone who could minister to them with understanding. *Those who have gone (and are going) through deep waters have a special opportunity for encouragement in the Body of Christ which will command God's unusual blessing.* With it comes a great and glorious reward (Heb. 10:35).

The apostle Paul, speaking from personal experience, sums up this side of God's purpose in temptation with this beautiful passage:

> Thank God, the Father of our Lord Jesus Christ, that he is our Father and the source of all mercy and comfort. For he gives us comfort in our trials so that we in turn may be able to give the same sort of strong sympathy to others in theirs. Indeed, experience shows that the more we share Christ's suffering, the more we are able to give of his encouragement. This means that if we experience trouble we can pass on to you comfort and spiritual help; for if we ourselves have been comforted we know how to encourage you to endure patiently the same sort of troubles that we have ourselves endured. We are quite confident that if you have to suffer troubles as we have done, then, like us, you will find the comfort and encouragement of God. (II Cor. 1:3-7 Phillips)

Yes, we live in a world which has fallen heir to God's judgment because of man's rebellion, yet there is a future expectation which shall be realized when redeemed man moves into the full power and authority of his sonship in Christ. There is a great wonder in these words from the apostle Paul:

> For I reckon that the sufferings which we now endure bear no comparison with the splendour, as

175

yet unrevealed, which is in store for us. For the created universe waits with eager expectation for God's sons to be revealed. It was made the victim of frustration, not by its own choice, but because of him who made it so; yet always there was hope, because the universe itself is to be freed from the shackles of mortality and enter upon the liberty and splendour of the children of God. Up to the present, we know, the whole created universe groans in all of its parts as if in pangs of childbirth. (Rom. 8:18-22 NEB)

The same passage in *The Living Bible* is also worth quoting:

Yet what we suffer now is nothing compared to the glory he will give us later. For all creation is waiting patiently and hopefully for that future day when God will resurrect his children. For on that day thorns and thistles, sin, death, and decay — the things that overcame the world against its will at God's command — will all disappear, and the world around us will share in the glorious freedom from sin which God's children enjoy. For we know that even the things of nature, like animals and plants, suffer in sickness and death as they await this great event. (Rom. 8:18-22 TLB)

How much more meaning the "wilderness" temptation of Jesus now assumes, *for as we follow in the footsteps of our Model Brother, we, too, can overcome on the very same "ground" which was the occasion for His victory.*

CONDITIONED FOR CONFRONTATION

Let us now move along in our study to another encouraging and revealing detail in the story: "And when (Jesus) had fasted forty days and forty nights, He afterward hungered. And the Tempter came . . . !" For forty days Jesus had been led of the Spirit throughout the wilderness. It was a time of intense testing, which demanded He be constantly alert and unceasing in His prayer. The flesh is easily weakened by spiritual warfare, and Jesus became aware of the physical and emotional strain at the conclusion of the forty-day period. Perhaps, as anticipated by Elijah's experience, He had been living on the strength of His Father's Word and Spirit, which He had received in a special way at His baptism. Now, physically and psychologically, He was exhausted and in great need of nourishment and rest. In the natural, He was both weak and weary!

Consider an analogy in the life cycle of hard-shelled crustaceans such as crabs and lobsters which periodically shed their exoskeletons (shells) for purposes of growth. A new shell then forms which serves both as an attachment framework for their muscles, and as a protective armor. During the molting phase, however, they are totally defenseless, soft-bodied creatures at the mercy of their environment. It is the most dangerous time in their life cycle.

All of us have experienced times of exhaustion when we have felt almost totally vulnerable and without defense. Like the little lobster, we have wished we could find a big rock somewhere under which we could hide for a little while and forget the world. Perhaps this is something of what Jesus felt when the Scriptures simply say, "And afterward He hungered!"

This was the precise time that Satan chose to confront Jesus with the three most challenging temptations in the entire forty-day period. *If Jesus as the Son of man can gain the victory here under these circumstances, then so can we be overcomers by following His example during our times of temptation.* Indeed there are striking parallels between the temptation of Jesus and that of Adam and Eve. Appeals were made in both cases for them to question the love, goodness, and integrity of their Heavenly Father. (The word "devil" literally means slanderer or false accuser.) If one was deceived at this point, the Devil knew doubt would develop and soon lead to outright disobedience. Both times, temptation touched sinless humanity (which was capable of not sinning) at possible entrance points: natural appetite, religious recognition, worldly ambition, and self-sufficiency. Each time, a bargain-basement crown was offered with no cross to pay. (Eternal crowns always contain fire-tested gold. Corruptible crowns are easy to come by, but are just as easily corroded.) The temptations were cleverly designed to induce humanity to substitute that which was earthly, temporal, and natural for that which was heavenly, eternal, and spiritual!

The temptation of Jesus was also a re-enactment of Israel's history. After their "baptism" in the Red Sea during the Exodus, the Israelites were led immediately into the wilderness where they were tempted and tried for forty years! (It could have been forty days if they had not doubted and disobeyed God.) Jesus clearly identified Himself with sinful humanity at His baptism, and we see that identification extended as He, too, underwent His wilderness temptation. (The many references by Jesus during His temptations to Israel's wilderness experience indicate how He Himself realized the close connection between them.)

178

The temptation account recorded by the Gospel must have come from the lips of Jesus Himself. How intently the disciples must have listened as the Lord shared His experience with them. He told them how very hungry He had become when He was confronted by Satan himself!

THE FIRST TEMPTATION

Let us look at the tactics of the Tempter and the divine defenses for victory which are available to us through Christ Jesus our Model Brother!

Satan initially challenged the Sonship of Jesus by suggesting He speak to the stones and turn them into bread, that He might appease His hunger: "If thou be the Son of God, command that these stones become bread" (Matt. 4:3). I am sure the disciples wondered what Jesus thought of the idea and how He responded. It really wasn't such an unreasonable suggestion. Certainly a kind and understanding Heavenly Father would hardly begrudge His beloved Son a loaf of bread following a forty-day fast! After all, it was God's Spirit that had led Him up into the wilderness in the first place. Surely it was obvious that He was weary and worn to the point of exhaustion and needed food.

At first they may have been surprised at the Lord's reply, for His only argument was a quotation from the Law: "Man shall not live by bread alone, but by every word that proceedeth out of the mouth of God" (Matt. 4:4; Deut. 8:3).

We don't know whether Jesus further explained the basis for His answer. Surely the Holy Spirit had given Him discernment and brought this portion of God's Word to His mind. The sword of the Spirit is the Word of God! (Eph. 6:17). Fortunately, the sword was in its scabbard! No wonder we are encouraged to hide God's Word in our hearts that we might not sin against Him (Ps. 119:11).

He may have pointed out to them that the issue really centered around whose word He would value the most. His Father, through the Holy Spirit, had permitted the wilderness experience for a purpose. Jesus had not yet been informed that the purpose was entirely fulfilled. *It was not Satan's prerogative to set the time for His fast to be broken, or his privilege to determine how it would be broken.* That waited upon a word from the Father. Where Adam and Eve had failed to wait, Jesus patiently waited! (Patience is one of the fruits of the Spirit which can be developed only through testing.)

Furthermore, it had been planned in the eternal council of the Godhead that although Christ Jesus had always been God, He would not cling to His rights as God, but would lay aside His mighty power and glory, and take the disguise of a slave and become like men (Phil. 2:6-7, TLB). *In other words, the Son of God would, as the Son of man, rely upon the same spiritual resources available to man rather than upon the privileges and power of His Godliness.* Only in this way could He truly be our example — a true Model Brother! Otherwise, it would not be fair for Jesus to "send us forth as the Father had sent Him" (John 20:21).

Jesus never played with divine power or perverted nature's purpose for His own needs or comfort. Even the breaking of bread for the five thousand was a merciful miracle for others, and a sign of His Sonship for them, not Himself. Also, it was bread that was multiplied, not stones magically transformed into loaves. The dignity and design of nature was not violated. Creation was respected by its Creator.

How different the story might have been if this

had been our temptation instead of His. It is so easy to rationalize our behavior when we have the power for self-satisfaction. "After all, forty days is a long time to give, even for God. We deserve to turn a little of our divine talent to our own welfare. This stone appears to be about the size loaf we are looking for. A little butter would be nice to spread on the bread while we are at it. Actually it might be a good idea to have a whole meal to go with our bread and butter. A forty-day fast really takes something out of a person.

"The sun is so terribly hot, perhaps we will command that cactus to become a palm tree. We will need some water, so we will just strike this rock and call forth enough to make a lovely pool as well. In fact, this would be an ideal place for an oasis — we can always turn it into a retreat center later on. It can be a sort of memorial to one's faith and obedience to the Lord. The world really needs a witness like this."

Such a fantasy may seem ridiculous on the surface, but if we probe deep enough into our hearts (and maybe our lives), I wonder if we would be surprised to find an oasis or two in the making? They sometimes are hard to recognize!

This is not to depreciate the need for true streams in the desert. Indeed, the desert is to blossom as a rose as rivers arise and ways through the wilderness are prepared. The roses, rivers, and highways are really people — *people, however, whose motives and means have been proven and purified through temptation and trial!*

A PASSAGE FROM THE OLD TESTAMENT

Further meaning can be found in the response of Jesus to Satan's suggestion by considering the Old Testament passage from which He quoted. It is found in the eighth chapter of Deuteronomy. It is suggested the entire chapter be read, but special reference will be made to the following verses:

All the commandments which I command you this day you shall be watchful to do, that you may live, and multiply, and go in and possess the land which the Lord swore to give to your fathers. And you shall (earnestly) remember all the way which the Lord your God led you these forty years in the wilderness, to humble you, and to prove you, to know what was in your [mind and] heart, whether you would keep His commandments or not. And He humbled you and allowed you to hunger, and fed you with manna, which you did not know, nor did your fathers know; that He might make you recognize and personally know that man does not live by bread alone, but man lives by every word that proceeds out of the mouth of the Lord. . . . Know also in your [mind and] heart that, as man disciplines and instructs his son, so the Lord your God disciplines and instructs you. So shall you keep the commandments of the Lord your God, to walk in His ways and (reverently) fear Him. (Deut. 8:1-3,5-6 TAB).

Jesus humbled Himself by willfully submitting to the wilderness temptations, that His faith in and obedience to God's Word might be fully proven. *To the Father it meant glory; to the Son it meant maturity of character; to Satan it meant defeat; to us it means instruction in righteousness.*

The first temptation is a lesson in establishing *priorities.* Jesus was faced with the decision of choosing between heavenly and earthly bread. He needed both! But for the moment He had to make a choice. It was a conflict staged by Satan between the spiritual and the natural, between the eternal and the temporal! The outer man is sustained by natural bread, but is destined to decay in time. The inner man is sustained by the Word of God, and is destined to live forever! Satan tried to deceive the Lord as he had Eve, by presenting the issue only in the light of a natural need, a need that could easily be met that minute by a single spoken word — from His own mouth!

"Thou shalt not eat of it" was the warning to Adam and Eve in regard to the forbidden fruit. They ate — and died! "Thou shalt not live by bread alone" was the Word of the Lord. Jesus obeyed, and now we may share His life. What a wonderful privilege it is to follow in His footsteps of faith and obedience. Truly He is our Bread of Life!

ESAU: A MAN WHO FAILED

Failures in Scripture are always presented as warnings which help us to more firmly fix the truth in our lives! A temptation somewhat similar in character to that which Jesus faced is recorded in the Old Testament. Sadly, the test was failed, and the consequences were tragic. Let us approach the story with the insights we have gained thus far:

One day Jacob was cooking stew when Esau arrived home exhausted from the hunt. *Esau:* "Boy, am I starved! Give me a bite of that red stuff there!" (From this came his nickname "Edom," which means "Red Stuff") *Jacob:* "All right, trade me your birthright for it!" *Esau:* "When a man is dying of starvation, what good is his birthright?" *Jacob:* "Well then, vow to God

183

that it is mine!" And Esau vowed, thereby selling all his eldest-son rights to his younger brother. Then Jacob gave Esau bread, peas, and stew; so he ate and drank and went on about his business, indifferent to the loss of the rights he had thrown away. (Gen. 25:29-34 TLB)

Later when Isaac, their father, was about to die, he desired to give his blessing to Esau his eldest son. The birthright of the first-born involved not only choice material blessings, but the covenant blessing God had promised to Abraham and his descendants. Esau had already sold his spiritual heritage for a bowl of soup! Jacob cunningly disguised himself as Esau and deceived Isaac into giving him Esau's blessing. The following scene unfolded as Esau returned not realizing what had just transpired:

(As soon as Isaac has blessed Jacob, and almost before Jacob has left the room, Esau arrives, coming in from his hunting. He also has prepared his father's favorite dish and brings it to him.) *Esau:* Here I am, father, with the venison. Sit up and eat it so that you can give me your finest blessings!" *Isaac:* "Who is it?" *Esau:* "Why, it's me, of course! Esau, your oldest son!" (Isaac begins to tremble noticeably.) *Isaac:* "Then who is it who was just here with venison, and I have already eaten it and blessed him with irrevocable blessing?" (Esau begins to sob with deep and bitter sobs.) *Esau:* "O my father, bless me, bless me too!" *Isaac:* "Your brother was here and tricked me and has carried away your blessing." *Esau:* (bitterly) "No wonder they call him 'The Cheater.' For he took my birthright, and now he has stolen my blessing. Oh, haven't you saved even one blessing for me?" *Isaac:* "I have made him your master, and have given him yourself and all of his relatives as his servants. I have guaranteed him abundance of grain and wine— what is there left to give?" *Esau:* "Not one blessing left for me? O my father, bless me too." (Isaac says nothing as Esau weeps.) (Gen. 27:30-38 TLB)

This incident is referred to by the writer of Hebrews. He uses strong words, filled with feeling, which convey a keen sense of caution to his readers:

> Aim at peace with all men, and a holy life, for without that no one will see the Lord. See to it that there is no one among you who forfeits the grace of God, no bitter, noxious weed growing up to poison the whole, no immoral person, no one worldly-minded like Esau. He sold his birthright for a single meal, and you know that although he wanted afterwards to claim the blessing, he was rejected; for he found no way open for second thoughts, although he strove, to the point of tears, to find one. (Heb. 12:14-17 NEB)

Now we clearly see what would have been lost if Jesus had failed in the first temptation. *He would have lost His inheritance, and since we are joint-heirs with Him (Rom. 8:17), we would have lost out as well!* Paul's comments concerning our joint inheritance indicate the weight which rested upon our Lord's decision in that crucial hour:

> For God has allowed us to know the secret of his plan, and it is this: he purposes in his sovereign will that all human history shall be consummated

in Christ, that everything that exists in Heaven or earth shall find its perfection and fulfillment in him. And here is the staggering thing — that in all which will one day belong to him we have been promised a share (since we were long ago destined for this by the one who achieves his purposes by his sovereign will! (Eph. 1:9-11 Phillips)

That would be a lot to lose — forever! How thankful we can be to the Lord Jesus for His unswerving faithfulness to His Father's will. Our destiny was involved!

THE SECOND TEMPTATION

Undoubtedly the disciples were held spellbound as Jesus proceeded to tell them that Satan then led Him to Jerusalem and set Him on the pinnacle of the temple. I am sure they wondered what kind of a temptation could arise in the midst of such a high and holy setting. The Lord then informed them of the very words which the Devil chose to use in his endeavor to entice Him to presume upon God's grace:

If thou art the Son of God, cast thyself down: for it is written, He shall give His angels charge over thee: And in their hands they shall bear thee up, lest at anytime thou dash thy foot against a stone. (Matt. 4:6; Ps. 91-11-12)

(Matt. 4:6; Ps. 91:11-12)
Satan is not omniscient! He does not know how we will handle the suggestions he would place in our hearts and minds. He employs a try-and-see technique based on our past responses to temptation. He is an expert in human nature and cleverly adjusts his approach in an endeavor to detect and exploit any

area in our lives which might be susceptible to his subtle suggestions. Having failed in a rather direct and even crude attempt to overcome Jesus at the sensual level of physical gratification, he then moved in a far more sophisticated fashion.

The scene changed from the dismal setting of the desert to a lofty position on the holy temple in Jerusalem. What an interesting study in contrast: the disorderly array of misshapen rocks in the wilderness is replaced by the beautifully shaped and carefully placed stones of the temple. Instead of the lonely desert, we see busy streets filled with voices clamoring for attention. Perhaps the Tempter thought a change in setting would prove advantageous to his purpose. Since Jesus had resisted the first temptation by giving priority to that which was holy rather than that which was earthly, Satan moved the setting for the next temptation into the Holy City itself. Before him were the very people whom the Lord wanted to reach with the Good News of the Kingdom. They were waiting for their Messiah. Malachi had prophesied that He would come suddenly to His temple! (Mal. 3:1).

The Tempter's tactics change as our level of spiritual maturity and responsibility progresses! He will appear as an angel of light in the midst of our noble intentions for God. He may even disguise his endeavor by quoting Scripture, realizing the respect and confidence we place in God's Holy Word. He is a master of both mutilation and misinterpretation of Sacred Scripture. The passages he will use are taken out of context and mis-applied. They are often misquoted or half-quoted, thereby perverting the very purpose of the record.

Since Jesus had relied upon the power of God's Word in resisting Satan's first attack, the Tempter now cleverly employs the same technique, even using

187

the very words Jesus had spoken: "It is written!" The devil actually believes he can deceive Jesus and entice Him to prove His power as the Son of God before the sons of men. Satan does not have the power or authority to push Jesus off the pinnacle himself, but he hopes to achieve the same end by tempting Him with a promise from Psalm ninety-one, which has been subtly disconnected from its qualifying conditions.

God's care and angelic protection are only for those who:

1. Dwell in the secret place of the most high (91:1, 9)
2. Confess the Lordship of their God (91:2, 9)
3. Set their love upon God their deliverer (91:14)
4. Know the lifting power of God's name (91:15)
5. Call upon God in time of trouble (91:15)

This is a picture of a man who walks closely with God, continually submitting himself to His wisdom and will. His great desire is to love God and follow Him in faith and obedience. He does not test God as a condition for his trust, but believes in Him and thereby finds protection and direction in all his ways. Jesus was aware of the context from which Satan had isolated his quotation but didn't even bother to correct his faulty interpretation. He struck instead at the ultimate and hidden purpose of the temptation which the Devil had hoped to cleverly conceal: "Thou shalt not tempt the Lord thy God!" was the Lord's reply, and the real issue was clearly defined. *You don't test those whom you trust!* Jesus didn't doubt His Father's wisdom or His faithfulness. Nor did He need a sign to prove His own Sonship to Himself or others. Signs there would be, but at the time and place of His Father's choosing.

PASSAGE FROM THE OLD TESTAMENT

Once again Jesus selected a passage related to the wilderness wanderings of the Israelites (Deut. 6:16, Exod. 17:1-7). They had arrived at Rephidim and discovered there was no water. Rather than standing in faith with Moses, trusting God to supply their need, the people murmured and complained. How quickly they had forgotten the Lord's provision of manna and quail during a previous food shortage! Now they were tempted to doubt. Moses was instructed to strike the rock at Mount Horeb, and life-giving water gushed out in sight of the elders of Israel that the people might drink.

An interesting comment is then added to the record:

He [Moses] called the place Massah (proof), and Meribah (contention), because of the faultfinding of the Israelites, and because they tempted and tried the patience of the Lord, saying, Is the Lord among us or not? (Exod. 17:7 TAB)

How easy it would have been, in our eyes, for Jesus to have listened to Satan. For forty days the heavens had been closed and silent. The heavenly dove had been replaced by the vultures of the desert. Perhaps it was time for the Father to re-affirm the Sonship of Jesus. To leap onto the courtyard below just as the priests presented the morning call to worship would certainly be to make a sensational entrance into the religious system of the day. Such a miraculous performance would satisfy the messianic expectations of the people. One master miracle like this, coupled with an immediate backroom conference with the religious leaders to assure them of their part in the Kingdom, would have established His position among the people forever! Or would it?

Faith and confidence which are based on miracles and signs alone require additional and greater wonders to keep one satisfied! As with the children of Israel, more and more signs would be needed to keep proving the presence of Deity. This is an "if we see, we will believe" philosophy. The Lord clearly established the proper priority for men of faith during His discussions with the disciples following His resurrection.

> Blessed are they that have not seen, and yet have believed. (John 20:29)

Jesus further indicated that signs are to follow the believer rather than the believer following after signs! (Mark 16:17,20). The apostle Paul, speaking from experience, expressed the principle most precisely: "We walk by faith, not by sight!" (II Cor. 5:7). Jesus never performed signs and miracles to gain the favor or approval of the religious leaders. He never used wonders to obtain and maintain the support of the crowd. In fact, He sometimes purposely disappointed the people when He sensed their interest in Him was more for His miracles than His message. There is ever a danger for signs and wonders to become ends in themselves, when they are only a means to an end. *Their purpose is to bring man to a place of commitment to God's will!*

The Lord Himself is the greatest sign! Fulfillment in life can only be found in following Him in faith, love, and obedience. True discipleship is the foundation for the Kingdom of Heaven. This involves a purity of heart and motive which expresses itself in life and practice. Jesus was not deceived by the Tempter's tactics. His first visit to the temple was going to be under very different circumstances from these dictated by the Devil. The money changers would soon discover this for themselves! The Jews were going to be given a sign, but one far different than they expected! (John 2:13-22).

Jesus was not presumptuous! He did not assume the favor and protection of His Heavenly Father would cover an action that had not first met with His approval. The Father, indeed, would confirm again and again the power and authority given to His Son, but this was not the time nor the place for the beginning of the Lord's earthly ministry. Satan had said, "Prove your Sonship by jumping." Jesus proved it by His refusal to jump. Again the Devil had failed.

SOLOMON: A MAN WHO FAILED

I am sure the Tempter was surprised. The same approach had worked before. Perhaps the design of this temptation had been based on an earlier victory over another man chosen of God. As the son of a great king, he, too, had inherited great power and authority. His name was Solomon! It was to be his privilege to build the holy temple. It was to be a beautiful edifice, symbolic of God's presence among His people. It was designed as a worship center around which men could experience God's love and forgiveness. Here they would be instructed concerning His holy purpose for their lives. United, they could present a loving witness of God's grace as it was to extend to all nations (Gal. 3:8).

What began with such bright promise, however, ended in division, hostility, and tragedy for the kingdom. Someone failed, and that someone was Solomon! How was he tempted to miss God's purpose, even in the very shadow of the temple which was constructed during his reign? God had given him a great gift of wisdom, which brought to the kingdom both wealth and glory. But then, sadly, the story changed, for in his heart Solomon began to presume upon God's goodness and love.

In I Kings 11:4 we are told that Solomon's heart was not perfect with the Lord as was the heart of David his father. His prayer of dedication for the temple concludes with an interesting statement:

> O Lord God, turn not away the face of [me] Your anointed one; [earnestly] remember Your good deeds, mercy and steadfast love for David Your servant. (II Chron. 6:42 TAB)

The Amplified Bible has a most revealing footnote concerning this passage. It raises the question of how young Solomon, obviously sincere in his prayer, could have subsequently fallen into a pattern of life which utterly defied the will of God in spite of explicit commands and warnings. *It is suggested that perhaps Solomon in his prayer was informing God that it was His responsibility to keep his face turned toward the Lord for His own sake, thereby relieving himself of any sense of accountability.* If such were his attitude, God rather abruptly clarified the issue for him concerning obedience and personal responsibility through a divine visitation in the night (II Chron. 7:12,17-22). Sadly, there is no evidence that Solomon took God's admonition seriously. He seems to have considered himself exempt from the commands of God — an attitude which can lead only to disaster!

LESSONS FROM LIFE

The application of our Lord's second temptation to our own lives is most practical. A young lady once requested I agree with her in prayer that she would remain true to a revelation she felt God had given to her. The prayer group of which she was a part had expressed some concern over the matter. It seemed wise to inquire further before praying, and in the process, the whole story unfolded. Through a series of impressions, coincidences, and "confirmations" from the Word, she was convinced that God had revealed to her whom she was going to marry and what the date would be. The young man was a rather prominent TV personality in evangelistic circles. He knew nothing of her interest. Furthermore, she was confident she could not be deceived because she and her sister had bound Satan and claimed God's protection just as the Scriptures indicated was the privilege of those who believe and agree in the name of Jesus (Matt. 18:18-20). She had taken her stand on the basis of God's Word! She was honest and sincere and obviously loved the Lord very much.

The Enemy, however, had sought to deceive her concerning the way in which she thought her protection would come. She presumed, after confessing the sure word of the Lord, that automatically every thought and impression would be of God. The Scriptures also indicate, however, that there is safety in a multitude of counselors, and we need to submit to one another in Christ Jesus (Prov. 11:14). *Sometimes divine protection and direction come through the counsel of more mature and discerning members of the family of God!*

I shared this truth with her, and suggested that possibly God was answering her prayer through our visit together. We realized that should her impression truly be of the Lord, all concerned would joyfully know in a matter of days. If it wasn't, God in His grace was forewarning her that Satan was hoping to destroy her faith through disillusionment. She considered this possibility, but I sensed she was still a little uncertain. I then related to her a most amazing coincidence which I am sure was really providential. Some weeks earlier another young lady had shared a very similar story with me — and it involved the very same young man!

The succeeding weeks proved the wisdom of divine providence, for no marriage was forthcoming. The Lord had not only prepared one of His handmaidens for what might have been a cruel and crushing blow to her confidence in God's Word, but a valuable lesson had been learned concerning the subtle ways in which Satan would even seek to snare the saints with Scripture. If our hearts are submissive, however, the Holy Spirit will be faithful to apply the *whole* counsel of God and His Word to our lives so we need not fear.

God often uses times of testing and temptation as a means of forcing to the surface of our lives hidden streaks of sinful self that need to be faced in the light of His forgiving and overcoming love. Years ago I received an invitation to participate in a charismatic witness meeting. It was a banquet setting, and the coordinator indicated it could also be an announcement and autograph party for the recent publication of our first book. God definitely impressed me this was not the direction He wanted for that meeting, so I declined, although both my wife and I had looked forward to the fellowship. We had calculated that with the baby-sitter and meal tickets, the cost of the evening would come to about ten dollars, which for our budget was of some significance.

Some days later I received an anonymous letter from a lady who simply said she felt impressed to send to us a gift of ten dollars. I was pleased, but remember telling my wife I wondered why God had moved in such an unusual way. We could always use ten dollars, but we weren't really lacking for food or necessities. Then I remembered our proposed banquet meeting. We had really wanted to attend but I had thought the circumstances had ruled out the possibility of our going. Now I had a strong inner witness that we should go, but how could I explain my change of mind and also obey God in light of the book situation.

I put off a decision, not knowing just what to do, until the last day the mail service could get the letter of explanation to the coordinator. In fact, I was still wondering what to do or say half an hour before the last postal pickup. Then it happened! I began complaining to the Lord for getting into such a predicament. I wanted to do His will, but all my desire had done was to get me into an awkward situation. Did God want me to go or didn't He? If He really did (and I was pretty sure He did), how was I going to explain my reversal of thought to my host without offending him?

I recall walking back and forth in the living room, becoming more and more agitated with every tick of the clock, until what had been on the inside finally exploded. With great intensity of feeling, I informed the Lord that if He was the Good Shepherd He said He was, He had better start leading me in a hurry, because I didn't know what to do and there wasn't much time in which to get it done! I was horrified to hear with my own ears what I had just said. I rather quickly told the Lord I didn't really mean it, and that I was sorry that in a moment of pressure I had been presumptuous.

Repentance has a way of bringing us to a place of holy quietness before God! Then came a very clear impression from the Lord. It was in the form of a question. "If I really believed I had the mind of Christ, what would I be doing now?" I replied, "I would be writing my letter!" Immediately the Lord responded, "Well, why aren't you?" With a sense of assurance, I went to my desk, headed my letter, and began to write. As I did, the gracious thoughts of the Lord flowed in a most perfect and pleasing way. Furthermore, the direction of the Lord was evident in the meeting that followed. An unusual opportunity developed which God blessed in a most meaningful manner. I had a particular ministry to give which helped fulfill His will — but in His way! *God had redeemed my presumption, but only after I had brought it to Him in repentance!*

The Lord still reminds me of this incident whenever I am prone to murmur and complain because I don't see far enough ahead concerning the specifics of His will for my life. He really is a Good Shepherd, and His sheep will know His voice *if they are quietly following in faith and obedience.* No wonder the devil would tempt us to doubt and disobey. How thankful we can be for the discerning and delivering power of the Holy Spirit during our times of trial and testing. The rod of His protection and the staff of His direction are truly a source of abiding comfort!

THE THIRD TEMPTATION

It must have been most disconcerting to the devil to see Jesus not only resist, but triumph over, the temptations he had so carefully and cleverly designed. These approaches had worked so well in times past that he had developed a great confidence in his deceptive devices. He knew the weaknesses of human nature, and now that Jesus had assumed the limitations of humanity, Satan was sure it was only a matter of time and testing and he would discover a weakness in character which would bring Jesus to His knees in defeat.

It never occurred to the Adversary that he himself was deceived and deluded. In his original rebellion against God, pride had so darkened his mind that he actually believed he would be victorious. Indeed, he persuaded many of the heavenly host to join with him in his attempt. *The seeds of delusion are inherent in pride.* Satan was actually self-deceived into thinking that ultimately evil would overcome good, error would triumph over truth, and love of self would overthrow love for others!

The Tempter's third approach was based on the assumption that there was an element of hidden pride in the Lord's life which was strong enough to bring Him into Satanic submission. *How easy it is to project a hidden weakness in our own life into that of another!* The character of the third temptation is by far the most powerful and significant of all. So closely is it related to the character of the Tempter himself, so basic in thrust and encompassing in scope, it actually includes the essential elements of all temptations.

Jesus must have described to the disciples how the Devil had taken Him to the top of a very high mountain and in a moment of time had shown Him all the kingdoms of the world and their glory. Jesus *was* kingdom-minded. In Matthew's Gospel, The Lord is uniquely presented as the King of kings. The term "kingdom" is found over fifty times in the book. The phrase "kingdom of heaven" is also a favorite of Matthew and is used some thirty-four times. The kingdom Jesus came to establish was clearly a spiritual, heavenly and eternal one — the Kingdom of God. Indeed, it was to be expressed on earth, but its roots were established in heaven!

To Satan, power, glory, and honor were to be for one's own sake — not God's! Being deceived himself, possibly he felt this was a common ground of approach to the Lord. Jesus then related to the disciples the very words the Tempter used in presenting to Him his proposition:

> I will give you all this power and glory, because it was given to me and I may delegate it to anyone I please. Now if you will bow down and worship me, all of this will be yours! (Luke 4:6-7 various translations)

A PASSAGE FROM THE OLD TESTAMENT

The disciples must have sat in stunned silence feeling the Satanic force behind the statement Jesus had shared with them. Undoubtedly their eyes were fixed upon His face as they leaned forward to hear His reply. The words were strong and authoritative:

> Away with you, Satan! The Scripture says, "Thou shalt worship the Lord thy God and Him only shalt thou serve." (Matt. 4:10 Phillips; Deut. 6:13)

The Old Testament context from which this passage is chosen is most beautiful and exceptionally interesting (Deut. 6:1-15). Moses had just presented the ten commandments to the children of Israel. The purpose of the law was to provide a framework for life in the promised land. They were to be a model people whose loyalty and love were completely centered in the Lord their God. Their entire ambition was to be set in doing and obeying God's will and providing an example to the world around of His love and wisdom.

The Lord wanted His people to love Him with all their heart and soul and might!

Their primary orientation was to be heavenly, not earthly; upward to God, not outward to the world. The Lord knew that what they set their affections and ambitions upon would determine their direction of worship. He warned them not to be allured by the gods of this world, for He was jealous for His people. God's redemptive plan and purpose for mankind rested upon their willingness to lovingly trust and obey Him without reservation. This is the thought and feeling conveyed in the passage which Jesus quoted.

Israel had failed in their mission. The whole matter had now shifted from a people to a *Person*; from many to One Man. Upon His shoulders alone rested God's entire redemptive purpose. As was Israel, He, too, was being tempted concerning the crucial issue of worship!

Inherent in worship is the concept of "worth-ship"! The word "worship" is related to that which we consider to be of supreme worth. Worship is characterized by its object. The object of our worship is in turn determined by our values. Therefore, we worship that which we consider in our own estimation to be ultimately worthwhile. Everyone has a system of values to which they submit and commit their lives. It is not a question of *whether* we shall worship, but *what* we shall worship. Everybody is a worshiper!

Destiny is determined by worship! What we worship is indeed the "ultimate issue of the universe," as T. Austin-Sparks entitled one of his fine books. We are free to choose what we shall worship, but once we do, it becomes our master for the future. In other words, we are mastered by what (and whom) we worship! Ultimately, *what* we worship is related to *whom* we worship. There are the values of Satan and the values of God. We decide to what and to whom we shall submit our lives.

Satan's desire is that we serve only ourselves, and in so doing his will, we pay homage to him. Earthly glory, honor, attention, power, and prestige are all promised to the person who centers his desire in himself. There is a price tag, however; the lordship of Satan! Notice the Tempter's proposition to Jesus: "All of this will belong to you, if you will belong to me." Many have been deceived into buying such a line of goods, not realizing the purchase price involved.

A POST-WILDERNESS TEMPTATION

The Scripture declares that following the wilderness temptations, the devil departed from Jesus "for a season." There were various occasions in the ministry of Jesus which undoubtedly were designed by the Tempter for His undoing. One rather obvious account closely parallels the theme of the third temptation which we are now considering. The story is from Matthew 16:21-26. Jesus had just commended Peter for his strong confession concerning His divine Sonship. The Lord then indicated the necessity of His forthcoming death in Jerusalem. With great feeling and intensity, Peter reproved the Lord for even suggesting something as personally tragic and unfulfilling kingdomwise. Peter's love for Jesus was deep, and his desire to see the kingdom established was sincere. He failed however, to see the necessity of the earthly cross before the crowning of the Heavenly King.

The Lord's response involved a rebuke to Satan followed by instruction for Peter and the disciples concerning that which is of eternal value. Here is the record according to Saint Matthew (16:23-26):

"Out of my way, Satan! . . . You stand right in my path, Peter, when you look at things from man's point of view and not from God's."

Then Jesus said to his disciples: "If anyone wants to follow in my footsteps he must give up all right to himself, take up his cross and follow me. For the man who wants to save his life will lose it; but the man who loses his life for my sake will find it. For what good is it for a man to gain the whole world at the price of his own soul? What could a man offer to buy back his soul once he had lost it?" (Phillips)

Jesus knew whereof He spoke. Satan had indeed offered Him the whole world — without the cross! He could have had an earthly kingdom for the duration of time. But such a betrayal of His Father's trust would have cost Him the Kingdom of Heaven which is not for a time, but forever. Furthermore, fellowship with the Father would have been broken. Worship of Satan would have involved submission and surrender to him as master. Jesus' own destiny as the Redeemer of all mankind could not have been fulfilled. We would be without a Savior; God's Kingdom would be without a king or a people. On that temptation turned God's entire plan of the ages, for He has ever wanted a family whose faith, love, and obedience reflect that of their Elder and Model Brother, the Lord Jesus!

I am sure the disciples appreciated their Lord in a new way after learning all that was involved in the proving of Christ's perfect character prior to His earthly ministry. Some believe the temptation story may have been shared with them sometime during the forty-day period before the Lord's ascension. Certainly the account took on a much deeper meaning after the crucifixion for all of the disciples — except for Judas Iscariot!

JUDAS: A MAN WHO FAILED

Judas faced the same kind of temptation, but didn't discern the voice of the Tempter. Judas was a man pulled in two directions. There was something about Jesus that deepened his desire for spiritual and eternal values. Increasingly it became apparent, however, that the price for their reality in his life would involve the cross — his cross! It meant dying out to his own earthly ambitions and selfish desires. An earthly kingdom in which he would find a favored position of riches and honor was of supreme value in his estimation of life.

Jesus had warned His disciples that it was impossible to serve two masters, for eventually we would come to love one and hate the other. He applied the principle to an endeavor to serve both God and mammon (Luke 16:13). The term "mammon" is derived from a common Aramaic word for earthly riches or treasure. The idea behind the term involves not just gold or money, but any earthly value which is more precious to us than God Himself. Involved in the concept is a basic sense of security or trust. *We commit and submit our lives to what we feel is ultimately worthwhile and trustworthy.*

Judas was increasingly annoyed by the way Jesus would turn away and even offend the people every time they were ready to receive Him as an earthly king. The miracle powers of Jesus were seen by Judas as a way to win the approval of the people and establish an earthly kingdom characterized by health, wealth, power, and prestige. As a disciple, he was practically guaranteed a place of prominence when the time would come. As the trusted treasurer of the disciple band, he would undoubtedly hold a post in the realm of finance!

Already he had yielded to the temptation of withholding funds for himself from the money box in his care (John 12:6). The Lord's ministry was one of blessing, and Judas was not above exploiting the generosity of those blessed. One wonders if he may not have employed some little fund-raising schemes on the side to enhance the financial situation. His future in the Kingdom was, in his estimation, most promising.

When it finally dawned on Judas that the primary purpose of the Lord's ministry was not the establishment of an earthly kingdom, he was totally disillusioned and shaken in his soul. Bitterness and resentment took root and further spoiled his relationship with Jesus and his fellow disciples. An inward separation of heart removed him from the protection of their fellowship, and he tragically opened himself to the Tempter. Satan filled his heart with despair. His personal ambitions and bright dreams faded away into a meaningless mist. His god was gone, and now there was no shrine at which to worship. Jesus was no longer the light of his world, and the night was very dark indeed!

Judas not only sold his Lord for a paltry thirty pieces of silver, he sold his own soul for the same price. He lost what he sought to save! He later tried to undo what he had done by throwing the coins at the feet of the high priests, but all the silver in the world could not redeem his soul. Only Jesus could have done that. In betraying the Lord, he had deliberately cut himself off from God's only means of grace. Too late he learned he had chosen the wrong master!

How important it is for us to seek the Kingdom of God rather than to fall heir to the temptation of establishing our own kingdoms. *There is something in all of us which wants to protect and project our own ministries!* At first we may be careful not to contrive for our glory or gain, but the heart is deceitfully wicked!

LESSONS FROM LIFE

Some time ago, a witness team was invited to Denmark to share the Lord in a variety of unusual situations both inside and outside the church. Several in the group felt their witness was not as effective as they had hoped. I was among them. Actually, we were all secretly comparing ourselves with each other, and thinking how much more the other person was being used of God.

Finally, during a time of prayer together, we began to openly share our feelings of failure. I recall confessing my own thoughts of discouragement. Immediately one of the younger men looked at me with amazement and exclaimed in front of everybody, "Boy, you just fell off your pedestal!"

My first inner reaction was that maybe I had been too honest and forthright and should have tempered (tampered?) the confession a little!

It dawned on me later what had happened in our relationship. I hadn't consciously or deliberately placed myself on a pedestal. (It was, however, some satisfaction to discover he had put me there!) On a previous occasion, God had used me to be a particular blessing to him. There was nothing wrong in this or in the encouragement his testimony had brought to me personally. (Goodness knows, we are not going to get much encouragement along these lines from the world or from the devil!) What was wrong, however, was my second thoughts concerning the self-revealing aspects of my confession to the group. Subconsciously I felt it was necessary to protect and promote my image as a recognized "man of God." Everyone knows recognized

204

"men of God" never get discouraged! (I remember it seemed to me everyone else had become spectacular, "skyrocket" witnesses for God, and I couldn't even get my little "sparkler" going. Later, as I indicated above, I discovered we all were thinking the same thing!) I suppose we all could have remained silent concerning our inner needs for prayer and spiritual help and have missed the whole purpose of our meeting.

Actually, as we honestly shared our needs with one another, we discovered how we all had been deceived by false feelings of failure, which I am sure Satan hoped would remain hidden. It was as we submitted ourselves to one another in Christ that His healing power was released in all of our lives. Each one of us left the meeting much wiser and much stronger in the Lord. The entire mission proved to be unusually blessed of God, who alone — rather obviously — received all the glory!

The Scriptures declare God will not give His glory to another — in the sense that it becomes theirs and not His (Isa. 42:8; 48:11). The Psalmist responds to this truth with some intensity of feeling:

Not unto us, O Lord, not unto us, but unto thy name give glory, for thy mercy and for thy truth's sake. (Ps. 115:1)

That is not to say that His glory will not rise upon us or be seen through us, but it is *His* glory! (Isa. 60:1-2, 20).

Whenever His ministry through our lives is graced by any of the more spectacular spiritual gifts (in the eyes of men), there will come the temptation to receive glory unto ourselves. Subconsciously we begin to identify ourselves with God's ministry through us and before long, *His* ministry has become *our* ministry! Everything is then evaluated in terms of how it will enhance "the ministry." Without realizing it, our *ministry* has become our *kingdom*, and all else revolves around the throne of our ambition. This is an abuse of God's gifts, and while the recipients of those gifts will be blessed, ultimately the ministry itself will lose the blessing of God. *The purpose of the gifts is to build up the Body of Christ through which the Kingdom of Heaven is to be expressed here on earth!*

Very simply, the gifts of the Spirit are to enhance the Kingdom of God, not the kingdoms of men. Indeed, God has His gifted ministers, but they seek not to establish earthly empires, but the Kingdom of Heaven. Their great desire is not to perpetuate their name, but to glorify God. How the Tempter would deceive us into thinking that the way of earthly ambition and recognition is the road to success, even for the will of God. Surely there is a "more excellent way"!

The apostle Paul indicates "the more excellent way" involves an attitude of love which is not selfish, conceited, or envious (I Cor. 13). These are marks of humility which allow us to be more interested in the Kingdom of God than *our part* in that Kingdom! Even as I write these words, the Lord impresses me this is a truth going far beyond what I have yet realized in my own life. It is so easy to substitute words for obedience. This probably is one of the greatest temptations a teacher of God's Word faces in his own personal life — perhaps its true for us all.

It is natural for us to want to rule and reign in the area of "our ministry" for God. However, to the extent our part of the Kingdom assumes greater value in our eyes than the Kingdom as a whole, that part really has become *our* kingdom rather than His. Without realizing it, we are worshiping our ministry, and in so doing are accepting the Tempter's offer for an earthly kingdom, and actually paying him homage! That is not to say that there will be no blessing of God upon His Word when it is presented in faith to those who hunger and thirst after righteousness. The Spirit will bless any ministry as much as He can because of God's love for the lost and needy. *However, if the foundation is wrong, sooner or later the ministry will fail and fall, although the fruit of the ministry will remain.* How great is God's grace!

The failure of a ministry does not always mean its name, structure or function will suddenly cease (although it may, as history reveals), but it no longer is blessed of God in regard to His ongoing purpose. It may continue for a while as a whirlpool of activity, but it is aside from the mainstream of God's Holy Spirit. This is true of our ministries as individuals or the corporate ministry of local groups or communities. It likewise applies to larger movements or institutions.

Many of our prominent institutions of learning began with the purpose of training young men and women to be Christian leaders in our society. This spiritual vision was eventually lost, however, as those in places of administrative responsibility placed more and more emphasis on earthly values and recognition than that which is heavenly and eternal. They have become kingdoms in their own right, but Jesus Christ is hardly their king! The prince of this world is their sovereign and, whether it is realized or not, it is to him that they pay homage.

How clearly the third temptation of Jesus brings these issues into sharp focus. As the return of Christ our King approaches, should not we who make up His Kingdom recognize the need to prepare the way for His coming? I am convinced there is to be an expression of Kingdom power and glory here on earth as a witness to those who would never otherwise personally consider the Lordship of Jesus. I realize the fulfillment of the Kingdom awaits the personal coming of the King, but there is to be a preview for the world to see now!

As loyal and loving subjects, we have the joy of confessing the Lordship of our Christ as He rules and reigns both in and through our lives. *People should come in contact with the King when they come in contact with us!*

The gifts of the Spirit are also means by which Christ's power and glory can be manifested to those outside the Kingdom. We are not to play with God's power or place His holy gifts in a theatrical setting. They are signs graciously given that men may see God's love in action. May we not obscure their vision of the King by our failure to "excel" in the expression of these gifts and thereby draw attention to ourselves.

Should the Tempter seek to entice us with the glory of earthly kingdoms and the praise of men, may we respond swiftly and strongly as did the Lord:

Get thee hence, Satan: for it is written, Thou shalt worship the Lord thy God and Him only shalt thou serve!

JESUS: GOD'S PATTERN FOR VICTORY

In review of the temptations of Jesus, it goes without saying that Satan must have been sadly disappointed by his failure to find any ground of access into the Lord's life. Jesus expressed the strength and purity of His character in these words:

The prince . . . of this world is coming. And he has no claim on Me — he has nothing in common with Me, there is nothing in Me that belongs to him, he has no power over Me. (John 14:30 TAB) *Jesus not only resisted the temptations, but through the power of God's Spirit and the authority of God's Word, He actually triumphed over the Tempter!*

We have the same resources for victory as does our Model Brother. God has provided us with His written Word. In our encounter with Jesus as Savior and Baptizer in the Holy Spirit, we have received both His life and His power, and have become new creatures in Him. We have a new heart and a new mind with which to rule our lives.

It is true the potential for soulish, carnal behavior still exists, but through the power of the Holy Spirit we can continually put to death our lower nature. *It takes the power of the Spirit to "die daily," but the cross is also the gateway to victorious Christian living!* (Rom. 8 TAB). Our lower nature (soulish function apart form spiritual control) is the source of the "works of the flesh" listed by Paul in Gal. 5:19-21 (TLB):

> But when you follow your own wrong inclinations your lives will produce these evil results: impure thoughts, eagerness for lustful pleasure, idolatry, spiritism (that is, encouraging the activity of demons), hatred and fighting, jealousy and anger, constant effort to get the best for yourself, complaints and criticisms, the feeling that everyone else is wrong except those in your own little group — and there will be wrong doctrine, envy, murder, drunkenness, wild parties, and all that sort of thing. Let me tell you again as I have before, that anyone living that sort of life will not inherit the kingdom of God.

To entertain such sinful desires or engage in such sinful activity is to give place to the Tempter. Paul warns us not to allow the devil the opportunity to get such a foothold (Eph. 4:27).

To be forewarned concerning the Devil's strategy is to be forearmed. We have the same powerful weapons of *God's Spirit* and *God's Word* that Jesus had. It is our responsibility to use them. This requires an exercise of our will, regardless of how we feel at the time. This is how we become men and women of faith and obedience. Our part is to first submit to God's Son, God's Spirit, and God's Word; then we can successfully resist and rebuke the devil himself, and on the authority of Holy Scripture, he will flee! (James 4:7).

My first teaching assignment after going into the field of Christian education was very time-consuming. Ordering laboratory equipment, outlining courses, and counseling students — along with administrative duties — left very little time for anything else. One Saturday afternoon I was baby-sitting our children while my wife was attending a ladies' meeting off campus. Upon her return, I planned to go back to the laboratory and prepare for the next weeks' classes.

I was waiting halfway patiently for the time of her expected arrival. It finally came and went without any appearance on her part. The passing moments grew into somewhat of a mountain of inner agitation and turmoil. I could see my wife upon the canvas of my imagination talking about all kinds of trivial things and gaily laughing with all of the ladies, completely oblivious to time and her domestic responsibilities. Resentment, anger, and self-pity became the fertile ground for the development of dark thoughts which began to possess my mind and heart. I carefully rehearsed what I was going to say and how I would deliver my "greeting" upon my wife's arrival. The words were sharp, well chosen, and cleverly calculated for their power to inflict pain and induce guilt!

At the very peak of my creative endeavors, I was annoyed by a rather spiritual thought which didn't seem to suit the occasion at all. It was as if the Lord suggested this might be the time to put into practice some very fine Sunday school lessons I had taught on the power of God's love. I wished the thought had not come. I had spent some time in polishing my "welcome home" speech, and I had a feeling the whole thing was about to be spoiled.

Temptations and testings always involve a point of decision. I did not feel God's love, nor in the natural did I want to, so possessive had my unlovely thoughts become. But the Lord promised a miracle of His power if I would be obedient to His Word. The step of obedience, incidentally, involved a commitment on my part to say absolutely nothing, and to be gracious in attitude when my wife returned. (I had been tempted to compromise and merely delete some of the sharper points of my speech, but leave enough to carry the message across. Apparently the Lord read my mind!)

I finally submitted to God's Spirit and confessed with my mouth my intention to obey the will of the Lord. To my amazement, the Enemy really did flee! He also took with him the dark depression and resentment that had possessed my life for the moment. My whole world was brought back into proper perspective, and His peace once more ruled in my heart (Col. 3:15). To celebrate my victory and put the finishing touches to this grand occasion of triumph, I remember I decided I would surprise my wife by doing the dishes before she got home! It turned out to be a glorious homecoming!

Yes, the temptations of the Spirit-filled Christ

have a very personal and practical application for the Spirit-baptized Christian. *It is a privilege which only Christians can enjoy — to deny ourselves, take up our cross daily, and follow Jesus.* It is a path which not only passes through the wilderness of temptation, but also leads up to the Mount of Transfiguration! Listen to the apostle Paul's voice of experience:

> But all of us who are Christians have no veils on our faces, but reflect like mirrors the glory of the Lord. We are transfigured in ever-increasing splendor into his own image, and the transformation comes from the Lord who is the Spirit! (II Cor. 3:18 Phillips).

Jesus Christ was triumphant through temptation because He faithfully and obediently relied upon the power of God's Word and God's Spirit. This is our guarantee of victory, too, for He has set the pattern for us to follow. "Come, let us arise and be on our way!"

To be filled with the Spirit is to be filled with power to triumph over temptation!

10

The Spirit of Holiness

The Greek word for holiness is "hagios." From the Latin root come the related English words, "sanctification" and "saint." The corresponding root word in Hebrew is "kadash." The range of meaning in English is found in the verbs: *dedicate, consecrate, sanctify, hallow, venerate, cleanse, purify, and perfect.*

To many people holiness and sanctification are practically synonymous with a narrow, gloomy, joyless type of existence. They tend to equate a holy life with a hollow life. Nothing could be further from the truth, and how Satan would desire to perpetuate this lie. To see clearly the blind and blurred areas in our understanding of true holiness, we must first look to Jesus and see the whole matter as related to Him. *The heavenly pattern of holiness for the earthly saint is found in God's Son.* He alone is *the* Holy One. Let us see what this means to us personally.

OUR CALLING AND OUR CONDUCT

The apostle Peter relates the holy life to our *call* and *to our conduct.*

213

Like obedient children, do not shape your lives by the cravings which were formerly yours in the time of your ignorance, but, in imitation of the Holy One who has called you, do you also be holy in all your behavior, since it is written, "You are to be holy, because I am holy." (I Pet. 1:14-16 Weymouth).

One morning some time ago when we were living on the West Coast, I was driving to school for my morning classes. On the way I passed the elementary school where our children were then enrolled. As I approached I heard a loud bell persistently and repeatedly ringing. At first I wondered what such an unusual sound at that hour of the day might mean. It then occurred to me that it was probably the fire bell for a safety drill. In a moment I would be turning the corner of the school, and the playgrounds would be in view where the children assembled during such practice sessions.

As I looked back, I saw the doors of the school open wide and hundreds of children rapidly make their way to their appointed places of safety. Everyone was assembling as had been previously planned. The purpose of the ringing bell was now most obvious — for them it was a lifesaving sound!

I began to respond to the experience in a rather unusual way as I drove on past the school. Tears came to my eyes and I was most moved within. True, my children were among those whom I had seen, but my emotional response was far beyond what one would normally expect. It was then that I realized that God was trying to speak to me. As I submitted to the Spirit of prophecy, the message came forth as if God Himself were speaking:

214

"My son, I, too, am calling, loudly and persistently that the saints might hear My voice and quickly respond. I DESIRE THAT IN THE COMING HOUR OF DANGER THEY MIGHT ASSEMBLY THEMSELVES TOGETHER AS THE HOUR APPROACHES. For yet a little while, and the yoke of the Enemy shall be destroyed by the anointing (Holy Spirit) that will rest upon their lives."

The word "saint" means a *called-out-one.* The primary requisite for sainthood is to hear the call of Christ and respond to His claims upon our lives. "My sheep *hear* my voice . . . and they *follow* me" (John 10:27). This is the simple twofold basis for the life of holiness. *To hear and to follow speaks of our calling and our conduct.*

JESUS IS OUR HOLY PATTERN

The door and the way to the saintly life is both straight and narrow. "Strait is the gate, and narrow is the way, which leadeth unto life" (Matt. 7:14). Note this passage is not referring so much to *a way of life* as it is to *the way to life.* Jesus is simultaneously the door, the way, and the life. He said so! "I am the Door. Anyone who enters in through Me will be saved — will live" (John 10:9 TAB). "I am the Way and the Truth and the Life; no one comes to the Father except by (through) Me" (John 14:6 TAB). There is only *one* true door, *one* true way, and *one* true life! The Bible narrows the range of possibilities by which we can find the true life of holiness to one; that one possibility is a person, and that person is Jesus Christ. The life of holiness is the life that Christ is. "Be ye holy for I am holy." *Sanctification is the process by which the Holy Spirit conforms us into the holy image of God's Son!*

215

The twofold pattern of calling and conduct is beautifully illustrated for us in the life of Christ. Jesus was a marked man from His birth. He was called to be the Savior of the world. Even the name Jesus Christ in the original languages refers to His Saviorhood and Messiahship. He was called to be a man of destiny. His life was lived with a divine sense of mission and purpose. Every minute of His life was meaningful. Every encounter He had with people was divinely ordered. Every circumstance of His life was charged with eternal significance. Everything pointed in one divine direction. His only desire and great delight was to fulfill the will of His Father. He set His face like a flint and allowed nothing to swerve Him from fulfilling His divine destiny.

The conduct of His life reflected the commitment of His soul. There was a discipline to each day which was related to the direction of His life. His motives were pure. His life was clean. His heart was perfect. He was moved with compassion but was never mastered by feeling. Communication with the Father was constantly clear. His life was perfectly transparent and never once was it clouded with the sin of self-ishness. The eternal purposes of heaven were ever so real that the temporal pleasures of the world never possessed His life. He was *in* the world but not *of* the world. He hated sin but loved the sinner. He sat with sinners but was never soiled by their sin. To touch His life at any time or in any place or with any one was to touch the holiness of God. Indeed He was the sinless Son of God. *Jesus Christ was absolutely and altogether holy!*

THE HOLY SPIRIT: OUR PURIFYING POWER

With great feeling we now respond to our Lord's

clear call to us, "Be ye holy, for I am holy." We are both amazed and humbled at such a high and holy calling. As sons of God we, too, have become marked men and women from the day of our spiritual birth! And as fantastic as it seems, our Lord emphatically declares that as the Father sent Him, so sends He us to live a holy life in a most unholy world. The implications of our calling can be as frustrating and discouraging as they are amazing until we realize it is going to be accomplished in His way, not ours.

Once again we are directed to the third Person of the Trinity. He is God's way to personal holiness. As His name implies, He is the very Spirit of holiness. *It is His ministry to progressively reveal and release the holiness of Christ in and through our lives!* An Episcopalian friend rather vividly expressed it this way: "After I was filled with the Holy Spirit, I soon discovered that He was just waiting to take His little broom and begin housecleaning."

As the light of God's Spirit shines fully into our lives, a lifetime accumulation of trash, dust, and cobwebs comes to our attention and His. He requests permission to clean up one area of our life after another. If given free reign, He works with amazing swiftness and most efficiently. His housecleaning tools are varied, and some are most unusual. In fact, at the time we may never even recognize them as such. It is only after all is done that we realize that another room has become clean and bright.

We never readily appreciate how many rooms, closets, and cupboards there are in these earthly temples of ours until God begins His work of cleansing. Some areas are so easily and quickly brightened up that we aren't even aware of the change until some time later. Then, to our surprise, we notice that some musty corner of our life that had been a little dark and dingy before is now fresh and clean. Other areas seem to require rather persistent scrubbing and, to our dismay, are easily soiled again. However, by quickly submitting to the purifying power of God's forgiving Spirit as soon as the stains of sin are discovered, we find even these parts of our lives becoming shining examples of God's perfecting power.

Occasionally the Holy Spirit will come to a closet in these lives of ours which is closed to His presence. Knowing that Jesus can never be completely at home in a life where forbidden areas remain, He kindly but insistently asks us for the key. To resist His persistent plea brings conflict and confusion into our lives. We quickly realize that we are facing a far greater issue than the particular one with which the Holy Spirit confronts us. The real issue centers in our professed Lordship of Jesus Christ. If we are not completely mastered by Jesus Christ, then He is not really Master at all — for us! *The Holy Spirit's deep desire for you and me is that Christ Jesus be Lord of all . . . all of you and all of me!*

HOLINESS IS A LOVE RELATIONSHIP

True holiness can never be cataloged as a list of dos and don'ts. *Rather holiness is an attitude of heart that lovingly recognizes the Lordship of Jesus Christ!* We become willing bondslaves of our loving Lord. We are as committed to Him through the bonds of love as He is committed to the will of the Father.

Real holiness is a love relationship! A wedding ring is a seal and a symbol of eternal and undivided love. It is a love gift from the groom to the bride. The Spirit of Holiness is Christ's love gift to His Bride. It is the seal of our holy union with Him in salvation. It was a costly gift, and Jesus paid the full price. He gave Himself, all of Himself, that we through the Holy Spirit might intimately and personally know the life and love of God. Jesus was utterly and completely broken that we might have unbroken communion with Him.

It all becomes so clear in the light of God's love. *Holiness is Calvary!* It is an all-out surrender to the love and will of God, that His life might find full expression through ours. How trite and trivial is the attitude that tries to calculate how far one can go without being labeled "worldly."

So often we have a tendency to logically construct an artificial list of worldly dos and don'ts as if holiness of heart could be measured by men's minds. God's standard of holiness so far transcends any yardstick that we might project that we would do better to look first to His Son before looking to the world. It is possible to become so possessed by the negative attitude of avoiding the world that we almost become more worldly minded than the sinner who unconsciously is a part of it. How much better to be so possessed by the love of Jesus Christ that we always aim to order our behavior in such a way as to continually promote His presence in our lives and the lives of others. He then becomes our standard of holiness. *The more His measure increases in our lives, the more wholesomely holy do we naturally become.*

To be wedded to God's Son speaks of a life of holy adventure! We have dedicated ourselves to the exciting purpose of knowing Him and sharing Him with others. We jealously guard against anything that would so possess our body, mind, or spirit that our daily communion with Him or witness for Him might become clouded or confused. This is a most exacting but divinely exhilarating way to live. This is life as it was meant to be!

A truly holy life is also a very lovely life! It is a life in which nothing detracts from the beauty of the indwelling Christ. Just as we would never display a magnificent work of art in a cheap, gaudy picture frame, so our lives must suitably frame the lovely portrait of our Lord. The sensitive Christian will be very careful concerning extremes in conversation, conduct, or dress. Our desire is to allow our lives to become an attractive setting for His presence.

The principles which we have just shared together have very practical, present-tense applications. As we yield our total being to the Holy Spirit, He will faithfully and progressively deal with various dimensions of our lives which need His sanctifying touch. To realize that God desires to freshen and cleanse new areas of our lives each day lends a holy excitement to our Christian experience. He doesn't always begin at the same place in each life, and we must be careful not to gauge the spiritual progress of others by the precise way in which He is working in ours. God begins where we are and with the areas of greatest need. Let us allow Him to do His work in His way in our lives and in the lives of others. If we continue to encourage one another in the Spirit, He will faithfully proceed with His perfect work.

What we think, say, and do; where we go; what we listen to and look at; how we budget our time and order our lives; even how we care for our physical bodies will all come under the silent scrutiny of God's Holy Spirit. With expectation we will listen to hear what suggestions He will make and how He will enable us to meet the challenge of the disciplined life.

We will soon discover that there may be some things that others can do that we cannot! We will be careful, however, not to judge others, remembering the converse is also true. Also, many things that now seem to be such a permanent part of our life may strangely lose their importance as better things take their place. God will continually be leading us from the harmful to the good, to the better, to the best. At each step we find new freedom and wonder why we previously were so attached to unessentials.

HOLINESS IS A PURIFYING HOPE

The theme of personal holiness takes on a timely significance when we see it related to the character of the Church just prior to our Lord's return. Paul shares with us the desires of the Heavenly Bridegroom that His Bride, the Church, should be sanctified, cleansed, and washed. In fact, she is to be presented as a glorious Church without blemish (Eph. 5:26-27).

The end-time Church is also going to be characterized as a militant church. She will be consecrated for the purpose of a great worldwide witness unto all the nations. ". . . then shall the end come" (Matt. 24:14). This twofold character of *purity* and *power* will be the result of the *sanctifying* and *unifying* work of the Holy Spirit who in these last days is being poured out upon all flesh.

As individual members of the Church, we should relate our lives to the lateness of the hour in a meaningful way. The secular world is certainly aware of the uniqueness of our atomic age. *The Bulletin of the Atomic Scientists* is a publication which is dedicated to the peculiar problems of our times. On the cover of every issue is the face of a clock, the hands of which are set at ten minutes to twelve. No one knows when the clock may strike, but there is an awareness that time may be shorter than we think. The newspaper headlines daily reinforce this feeling of uneasiness.

As Christians we are told that when the signs of

the end-time begin to appear, we are to look up, for our redemption draweth nigh. In other words, we are to lift our heads and be alert and allow the Second Coming of Christ to be a *purifying hope* which quickens our desire to redeem the time and live life with eternity in full view. Perhaps we need to feel the same sense of commitment to God's holy will as Jesus did when He realized His hour was fast approaching. *Our hour may be closer upon us than we realize!*

What a motivating and purifying hope the soon return of the Lord becomes to our daily lives. The Holy Scriptures would even indicate that we can hasten the day of His appearance by keeping our lives filled with His Spirit of purity and power. As we encourage others to be continually filled with God's Spirit, we are actually playing a necessary part in preparing the Bride of Christ for her Bridegroom! Surely in view of our times we can make Peter's admonition our daily prayer. "What manner of persons ought [we] to be in all holy conversation and godliness, Looking for and hastening unto the coming of the day of God . . ." (II Pet. 3:11-12).

THE URGENCY OF OUR HOUR

Recently my wife and I prayed that God would confirm the sense of urgency in our lives which we have associated with the soon return of our Lord. I felt almost compelled to request that God would answer our prayer within the week if it were His will. The next morning I received a letter in the mail from an attorney in Los Angeles who has recently been filled with God's Spirit. The Lord had awakened him at 12:25 A.M. a few days previously, and the Holy Spirit had given him the following prophecy:

"Now we must all work together in the Spirit. Call on each dear brother as the need arises. Tell your problems freely. Ask for counsel and guidance. When a dear brother calls you, respond without question. There is much to be done throughout the world. There must be a harmonious blending of the talents of all those blessed with the Holy Spirit. Each will have a special gift to contribute to this great undertaking in God's work in these latter days.

"The time is short I say again and again and again. These are not idle words. People must be made to realize this. You are to make this urgency known through those with the Holy Spirit. Then the message will fan out and reach all peoples everywhere. All must be given their chance to accept Jesus and the Cross before it is too late. *Stress the lateness of the hour in everything you do for the Lord and in all your testimony, preaching, and witnessing.* Those not saved must be reached by every method and means and channel available to man. They must be told of the shortness of time in which to make their decision for Jesus Christ, Savior and Redeemer. Talk of this message whenever you are able.

"Our Heavenly Father is grieved because many alive today will not be saved because they foolishly think there is ample time remaining for salvation. In this, I repeat, they are wrong. Time is very short. The day of reckoning is near. The fulfillment of the Divine Plan is nigh at hand. Let all heed and turn toward the Cross. Man's blindness to this message will be his undoing. His eyes must be opened, and the light of our dear Lord Jesus must shine through to his soul and consciousness. The Holy Spirit will lead and

223

guide in this movement of the Lord. Give Him free reign and surrender and be obedient to His instructions. This is a clear call for action by all Spirit-filled people everywhere to move in God's work."

Since this prophetic word was given, the Lord has twice impressed me in rather special ways concerning the urgency of our day and hour and our responsibility to redeem the time.

One night I dreamed I was seated in the biology laboratory where I was teaching. I was located about three rows from the front and was in the role of a student rather than that of an instructor. The teacher in my dream was not at the instructor's desk in a place of leadership as he should have been, but was seated back with the students to my left.

I remember I was speaking to the class, but it wasn't about biology; it was about Jesus! I was trying to convey how much the Father loves His Son and how He wants us to love Him, too. Furthermore, He desires that we express that love to each other and to the whole world and thereby prepare the way for His second coming.

It was with great feeling and conviction that these thoughts were being shared. As I was speaking, I felt as if there was very little response within the class. I looked around and everybody, including the instructor, was sound asleep with their heads resting upon their arms which were folded flat upon the tables. I wanted to cry out, "Wake up! Oh, wake up! How can you sleep at a time like this?"

In the morning I remembered the dream most vividly, and the Lord brought to my attention a related passage from Scripture. This same portion from God's Word was independently confirmed four times over by different individuals throughout the following week. It is found in Ephesians 5:14-18:

> Therefore, He says, Awake, O sleeper, and arise from the dead, and Christ shall shine [make day dawn] upon you and give you light. Look carefully then how you walk! Live purposefully and worthily and accurately, not as the unwise and witless, but as wise — sensible, intelligent people; Making the very most of the time — buying up each opportunity — because the days are evil.
>
> Therefore, do not be vague and thoughtless and foolish, but understanding, and firmly grasping what the will of the Lord is. And do not get drunk with wine, for that is debauchery; but ever be filled and stimulated with the (Holy) Spirit. (TAB)

The second time the Lord dealt with me in a rather special way was also in the night. I was clearly awake, and most sensitive to His still, small voice. I recall I was deeply impressed with the urgency of our times. The Lord indicated to me that He was going to be working more swiftly and extensively through His people than ever before.

Furthermore, I was impressed that God was going to be doing surprising things, in surprising ways, in surprising places, through surprising people. In fact, everyone would be surprised in one way or another! No one has the entire view concerning the magnitude of God's end-time ministry through His people. I was cautioned within not to imply to others that the part that I had perceived was the whole, nor was I ever to conclude that the vision anyone else might have would embrace the entirety of God's plan. In this way we remain humbly dependent upon the Lord and His ministry through each other.

As we continue to walk with Him in faith and obedience, He promises to reveal to us what we need to know concerning our role in His plan — as we need to know it. If we try to force our way into the future, apart from God's Spirit and His Word, we will only be giving place to a spirit of mystical speculation which inevitably leads into error.

In view of such exhortation from the Lord, may we daily consecrate and dedicate our lives to God's holy will without reservation. May we expectantly listen to His voice of instruction and then obediently follow our Heavenly and Holy Shepherd in the path of purity and power. *"Even so, come Lord Jesus!"*

To be filled with the Holy Spirit is to be filled with purifying hope.

11

The Spirit of Joy, Peace, and Love

THE JOY OF THE LORD IS YOUR STRENGTH

One of the streams of the Spirit which God is restoring to His Church is the river of joy. Indeed, the Holy Spirit Himself is a very joyful person! There are literally hundreds of references to joy in the Scriptures to confirm this observation. One of the strangest passages is found in Acts 13:52, where we are informed the disciples were full of joy and the Holy Ghost. What is odd about this reference is the context in which this joy was expressed. Paul and Barnabas had just experienced persecution at the hands of the "devout and honorable women and chief men of the city" and had been expelled from the area. Hardly an occasion for joy! Obviously it was not the setting that was the source of their joy, but an overflowing relationship in the joy of the Holy Spirit.

There is a principle here which applies to all of the fruit and graces of the Spirit: that is, they grow best from the ground of adversity. For instance, when the apostle Paul requested that his "thorn in the flesh" be removed, the Lord informed him that true spiritual *strength* is made perfect in the midst of human *weakness* (II Cor. 12:9). There appears to be a spiritual law of opposites defined here which indicates that *the heavenly streams of the Spirit spring forth most vigorously from the earthly ground of contrasting circumstances.* It is in restless times that we discover His rest; in turmoil, that we find peace; in irritation, that we know patience; in resentment, that we perfect forgiveness; and in distress, that we experience joy.

Jesus said we could be ever- and over-flowing Christians if we would continually trust and obey Him! (John 7:37-39; Acts 5:32). Once when my wife and I were undergoing a rather distressing time, the Lord used the occasion to further our understanding of this promise. We had just moved and had become involved in just about everything with which I vowed we would never again become entangled. It was necessary for my wife, who is a nurse, to work the three-to-eleven shift full time. I was endeavoring to establish a new science department, with many unforeseen disappointments. The evenings were hectic with the four children when their mother was away. Furthermore, we had just put in a new lawn on sloping banks which kept washing out with each thunderstorm! (I can still remember lying in bed and "rebuking the elements" as the first big drops of an impending storm began to fall. Somehow my frustrated faith never quite held the heavens back.)

One night the Lord gave me a dream in which I was among a group of people all of whom had just made a change in location. Someone suggested we all share what we felt the spiritual purpose was for our respective moves. My heart sank, for it was one of those times when you hope no one will call on you to pray.

228

When my turn came, my mind was distressingly blank until I opened my mouth in faith and in essence these prophetic words tumbled out: "This is a time of preparation in which each of us is enrolled in the school of the Spirit. We are not to face our daily afflictions with resentment, for this is the basic material God is using in shaping our lives into His image. Each day holds a heavenly lesson and an earthly exam. As we cooperate with the Master, it is our privilege to 'rejoice evermore, in all things.' "

Our joy and every other fruit of the Spirit does not have its source in our circumstances or from our feelings, but in Jesus. As we make this our confession, the Holy Spirit can bring a confirming witness to our hearts. There is something strong and steady in this kind of joy, because it is based on the faithfulness of the Lord rather than the fluctuation of our feelings or the uncertainty of our surroundings. As one man expressed it, *"It is a kind of solid joy, and it brings a staying power to our lives!"*

PEACE BE UNTO YOU

The fast, feverish, high-pressured pace of our modern world has produced an atmosphere which is not conducive to inner peace of heart. Far too often our lives are characterized by an inner agitation or restlessness of soul. Stress, strain, fear, and worry make their marks, and man's soul cries out for relief. It is even possible for the spirit of this age to spill over into our Christian life, and we can become so frantic in our service for the Lord that we succeed more in wearing ourselves out than in gaining solid ground for God in our lives or in the lives of others.

For the Spirit-filled Christian, however, there is the promise of inner peace and rest. There is a serenity of mind and repose for the soul which enables us to maintain a spiritual poise regardless of circumstances. Real life demands more than pretty promises and sweet sentiment. There must be a solid center to our lives which remains unmoved and untouched by the storms of life and the turmoil of our times. *That center is Christ!*

Let us explore this in a more specific way. Peace and rest are far more than just abstract characteristics of the Christian life. These words are more than just wishful thoughts or expressions of soft sentiment. Each one is a reference to something which is as solid as concrete and as strong as tempered steel. That something is really Someone. *That Someone is Jesus Christ!* Jesus Christ is what makes our Christianity concrete. When the Holy Spirit fills us with the Life of our Lord, He is putting steel into our soul. Peace is a Person; rest is a Person. *That Person is Jesus Christ!* He is the solid center of our lives!

Now we can only stay "on center" when we by faith allow the Holy Spirit to have full and complete control of our lives. If we are restless or lose our inner harmony of heart, we have moved "off center" in some area of our experience. All we have to do is ask the Holy Spirit to *recentralize* our lives. This He will do by many ways and means. Usually, He will simply begin with us, and suggest that we acquaint now ourselves with Him and be at peace (Job 22:21). It is impossible to get better acquainted with Jesus and not be at peace because — *He is peace!* It is the desire of the blessed Comforter to help us get better acquainted with Jesus just at such times as we need Him most.

The pathway of God's will is the pathway of peace! Here is a very positive principle that should give direction to every Spirit-filled believer. If any situation destroys your inner harmony of heart, quiet

230

yourself before Him. Ask the Holy Spirit of truth to reveal to you if something is off-center. It may be your doubts (misplaced faith). Ask God to square your faith with Scripture. Center your trust in His Word. To trust His Word when feelings and even reason may indicate otherwise will bring His peace.

On the other hand, your uneasiness may be a sense of discernment that Jesus is not finding the place He desires to have. Any situation which does not direct our full attention to the Lord is partially off-center. A truly Christ-centered life will quickly detect this. It may begin merely as a feeling of uneasiness, but as we seek God's Spirit to relate things to Jesus, He will bring discernment of a more specific nature!

The principle of peace finds very practical application when we face the many decisions which confront us in everyday life. *Every day is a day of decision!* Sometimes they are little decisions and sometimes big decisions that can change our entire lives. If we learn how to make the little decisions, we will know how to face the big ones. The way in which we face the decisions of today may well determine those of tomorrow.

For the Spirit-filled Christian, this way is the way of peace. Without inner peace of heart it is impossible to sense God's will or hear His voice. Sometimes His voice is very still and very small — purposefully so! The inner noise of confusion and unrest will completely drown it out. The remedy for such inner distress is simply the presence of Christ. One touch of His hand can calm the troubled waters of our soul.

I awakened one night greatly disturbed about the wisdom of a decision which I had made involving the entire family. The move had already been made, but I was plagued by worrisome afterthoughts. I have discovered that in the stillness of the night when all dis-

231

tractions are minimal, one can engage in almost pure, concentrated, and protracted worry! In fact, the Lord impressed me once that I was somewhat like a hound dog who, if tossed an old dead, dry bone, would immediately give it his complete attention. He would gnaw, turn, and worry that bone until he was worn out, but no nourishment was forthcoming whatsoever!

The Holy Spirit finally penetrated my hard head (and heart) with a word of discipline. "Why do you persist in re-opening doors that have been firmly closed in the past? Did you not make your decision in faith and obedience walking in all the light that you had? Was not your confidence in your Good Shepherd based on His faithfulness to ultimately guide you in the paths of righteousness in spite of your limitations? Did I not flood your life with the light of My peace at your time of decision? My Son, you have walked out of the circle of My light into the darkness of doubt. You then complain to Me concerning your confusion and pain. You are in a bed of your own making. There is nothing more that I can do other than point you once more in the direction of the light. The next move is yours!"

The thoughts were straight, strong, and somewhat stern — but life-giving and peace-restoring! I confessed how absolutely accurate the diagnosis had been, and the truth of God's Word immediately dispelled the dark clouds of worry and fear. How simply and sweetly the Psalmist touches our hearts with the same reassuring theme: "In peace I will both lie down and sleep, for You, Lord, alone make me dwell in safety and confident trust" (Ps. 4:8 TAB).

How easy it is for us to stray from the path of peace. But when we do we will hear behind us the call of our Blessed Comforter saying, "This is the way, walk ye in it" (Isa. 30:20-21). As our faithful Teacher of the Truth, He tenderly reminds us that the Lord Jesus Himself is the only way to peace with God, others, and ourselves. Upon returning to Him, we find inner rest — a divine quietness and confidence from which springs our strength for the day (Isa. 30:15). It is as we rest in the Lord that we can go forth in His name! ((II Chron. 14:11). Let us, therefore, better acquaint ourselves with Him and be at peace, for this is God's way to His goodness for us (Job 22:21).

And let the peace that Christ gives decide all doubts within your hearts — settle with finality all questions within your minds — for you were called to the enjoyment of peace as members of one Body. Learn to be thankful — appreciative, giving praise to God always! (Col. 3:15 various translations)

LOVE: THE HEARTBEAT OF GOD

What better topic could we choose with which to conclude our time in sharing together than that of love. God is love! We see His love expressed for us in Jesus. Calvary love is much more than sweet sentiment. It is the very heartbeat of God. *Love not only is; it gives!* The Father gave us His heart when He gave us His Son. He exhausted the very treasury of heaven that we might have fellowship with Him. In ourselves we are not worthy of His love, but He loves us anyway!

The love of John 3:16 is expressed by the Greek word "agape." It is the highest and noblest word for love. In the New Testament it takes on a divine dimension that gives it an infinite value. It is the kind of love that is characterized by the subject loving — God. It is further characterized by the value and preciousness of the object loved — you and me. God considers us to be of infinite value because of the divine purpose for which we were created — that we might be conformed into the image of His Son. *Agape love is Calvary love!*

The Holy Spirit is the Spirit of love. His overwhelming desire is to fill us with the love that God is. "For God's love has been poured out in our hearts through the Holy Spirit Who has been given to us" (Rom. 5:5 TAB).

THE LOVELY GIFTS OF GOD

The fruit and the gifts of the Spirit are expressions of God's love. The fruit of the Spirit (Gal. 5:22-23) is but a variation of love in its *being* or *character.* Love, joy, gladness, peace are what love is *within;* long-suffering, patience, gentleness, goodness are what love is *toward man;* faithfulness, meekness (humility), temperance (self-control) are what love is *toward God.*

The gifts of the Spirit as found in I Corinthians 12:8-10 are expressions of God's love in *thought, word,* and *deed.* Wisdom, knowledge, discernment are love in *thought;* prophecy, tongues, interpretations are love in *word;* faith, healings, miracles are love in *deed.*

To consider the gifts as expressions of God's life and love assists us in responding to the Spirit in faith when it comes to their manifestation. If we deliberately place ourselves before the Lord in expectation (choosing to be chosen), He has an available and cooperative vessel through which He can carry His love to another. *Our desire will be to share God's life and love, and actively allow the Spirit to minister through us in some specific way.* As we submit our spirit to His in faith, we will expectantly endeavor to think and feel as He would in our situation. As we become aware of His mind and affection, then it is our responsibility to express His will and feeling to God's people. This may also involve doing in faith what He would do if He were in our shoes — and He is! "As thou hast sent me into the world, even so have I also sent them into the world" (John 17:18).

Even those who through experience have learned "to excel" in the lovely expression of the spiritual gifts had to begin at the bottom. *There is a "first time" for everybody to try his spiritual wings.* The endeavor to put into words what we sense in the Spirit that God would say in a given situation can become sweetly inspired prophecy, a word of wisdom, or interpretation. Prayer in faith and in spiritual compassion (which is more than sympathy) can produce the climate for the demonstration of healings, miracles, and faith — all powerful expressions of God's love!

Some manifestations of the gifts seem to have a high order of inspiration and to be very sovereignly expressed. Other manifestations of the Spirit may occur or begin in what seems such a natural way we don't realize the inspiration involved until we see the obvious conclusion. Let us so live in the Spirit that God can move through us in the gifts whether we are aware of it or not. "A word fitly spoken is like apples of gold in pictures of silver" (Prov. 25:11). Here is a beautiful picture of a divine word of wisdom set in God's redeeming love. *May we be trees of life daily producing apples of gold for those who seek God's truth in love.*

Without the full complement of the fruit and gifts of the Spirit, God's love is incomplete to and through His Church. With the present outpouring of the Holy Spirit, we are seeing the Spirit of love completing His ministry in the Church. This is how the Church is to become as fresh and full of promise as the morning; as

235

fair as the still, cool beauty of the moon; as bright as the warm revealing sun; and as terrible as an aggressive victorious army with banners (Song of Sol. 6:10). *Love is fresh, fair, bright, and powerful!* Does not Calvary speak of promise, rest, light, and victory? This is the gospel of the Cross. This is our message to a hopeless, restless, darkened, sin-shackled world. Through His love God has provided deliverance for body, soul, and spirit. Can we do any less than shout to a dying world, "Look to His love and live!"

LONELY AND UNLOVED

Everywhere there are hearts literally longing for God's love! I recall several very vivid experiences related to this. One concerned a young seminary student who was interested in the Baptism with the Holy Spirit for his life. We had talked with him for a while and were about to pray together when he broke down and pleaded with me to pray that God would somehow reveal to him His love. I can still feel and hear the desperate cry of his heart as he longed to know that God loved him *personally*. The Holy Spirit prompted me with a word of wisdom which I immediately shared with him. "How could God any more clearly and forcefully show His great love for you, personally than He did when He gave His own Son? This makes you something special!"

Calvary love is terribly real, and he responded immediately to this real assurance that God graciously provided. How long he had carried this burden I do not know, but I somehow feel that there are many lonely lives, some whom we may least suspect, that are likewise longing for an assurance that God loves them.

A woman confided in me at the close of a meeting

that she never had truly known the love of God in her heart. She knew in her head He loved her and accepted that love at face value, but there never had been a warm witness within. She had endeavored as a Christian wife and mother to give and receive love to and from her family as best as she knew how, but it wasn't the genuine, heartfelt love she so deeply desired.

Upon inquiring, we discovered she had experienced very little love in her own family as a girl. She had always felt somewhat unloved and unwanted, although her family had provided her material needs. Unsure of the love of her earthly father, she found it difficult to understand the love of her Heavenly Father. She was a flower in the garden of God who had never bloomed because of a shadow from the past had shaded her from the warm light of His love.

I assured her that the releasing love of Jesus was going to set her free from childhood disappointment. Her Heavenly Father Himself was going to heal her heart and mind and fill her life to overflowing with His love. She was going to know it, and she was going to feel it! As we confessed the Lordship of our Christ, the heavy hold of the Enemy was broken, and God's releasing love flowed in. She sobbed away her sadness, and tears of joy gave evidence of a deep inner healing.

I told her she was going to enjoy a restful night of sweet sleep. After a crisis is past in sickness, the fever breaks and the "rest" of recovery is most pleasant. The same thing is true of inner healing. The warmth of God's healing love brings hope and joy to our days of convalescence. I was so happy to see her the next morning and to learn that indeed she had enjoyed a night of perfect rest and peace. God's love was now very real!

On another occasion I was counseling with the wife of a pastor who was interested in the fullness of

God's Spirit for her life. The Holy Spirit kept prompting me to assure her of God's love, but I was hesitant to tell a minister's wife something so basic. I didn't want to insult a well-trained and experienced handmaiden of God with such a simple and obvious truth. Finally I allowed the Lord to direct a prophetic word to her concerning His interest and love for her personally. To my amazement she cried out, "Oh, does God *really* love me? For a whole year I have been going through a valley of darkness and have wondered many times if God still loved me."

I realized then that to have continued our prayer and counsel for her Baptism in the Holy Spirit would have been fruitless, for this experience is entered into by faith. Love, however, is the source of faith and expectation. How can you put confidence in a God you are not sure really loves you? How wise was the Lord in reaching her primary need first. How careful we must be to obey His promptings!

CONCLUSION

There is no greater privilege than to share the love of Jesus with others! May His Spirit so fill our lives with the love of God that anytime, anyplace, anywhere, others may be able to look to us and know that God loves them. May we join with Rufus Moseley at this point and again repeat his rather charming comment, "Jesus really loves you, and He told me to tell you so!"

We now share with you this last thought, and really it is the most important of all for everything else rests upon it:

To be filled with the Holy Spirit is to be filled with Calvary Love!

238

Appendix

A CORRELATION OF SCRIPTURE RELATING THE PERSON OF THE HOLY SPIRIT TO THE LIFE OF THE BELIEVER

And ye shall seek me, and find me, when ye shall search for me with all your heart. (Jer. 29:13)

They received the word with all readiness of mind, and searched the scriptures daily, whether those things were so. (Acts 17:11)

I. PERSONAL PROMISES FOR HOLY SPIRIT BAPTISM

1. And it shall come to pass afterward, that I will pour out my spirit upon all flesh; and your sons and your daughters shall prophesy, your old men shall dream dreams, your young men shall see visions: And also upon the servants and upon the handmaids in those

days will I pour out my spirit. (Joel 2:28-29)

2.   In those days came John the Baptist, preaching in the wilderness of Judaea, And saying, Repent ye: for the kingdom of heaven is at hand. . . . I indeed baptize you with water unto repentance: but he [Jesus] that cometh after me is mightier than I, whose shoes I am not worthy to bear: he shall baptize you with the Holy Ghost, and with fire (Matt. 3:1-2, 11).

3.   He that believeth on me [Jesus], as the scripture hath said, out of his belly shall flow rivers of living water. (But this spake he of the Spirit, which they that believe on him should receive: for the Holy Ghost was not yet given; because that Jesus was not yet glorified.) (John 7:38-39)

4.   And I [Jesus] will pray the Father, and he shall give you another Comforter, that he may abide with you for ever; Even the Spirit of truth; whom the world cannot receive, because it seeth him not, neither knoweth him: but ye know him; for he dwelleth with you, and shall be in you.
    The Comforter, which is the Holy Ghost, whom the Father will send in my name, he shall teach you all things, and bring all things to your remembrance, whatsoever I have said unto you. (John 14:16-17, 26)

5.   But when the Comforter is come, whom I [Jesus] will send unto you from the Father, even the Spirit of truth, which proceedeth from the Father, he shall testify of me (John 15:26).

6.   Nevertheless I [Jesus] tell you the truth; It is expedient for you that I go away: for if I go not away, the Comforter will not come unto you; but if I depart, I

will send him unto you.

I have yet many things to say unto you, but ye cannot bear them now. Howbeit when he, the Spirit of truth, is come, he will guide you into all truth: for he shall not speak of himself; but whatsoever he shall hear, that shall he speak: and he will shew you things to come. He shall glorify me: for he shall receive of mine, and shall shew it unto you. (John 16:7, 12-14)

7. And, being assembled together with them, [Jesus] commanded them [the disciples] that they should not depart from Jerusalem, but wait for the promise of the Father, which, saith he, ye have heard of me. For John truly baptized with water; but ye shall be baptized with the Holy Ghost not many days hence.

Ye shall receive power, after that the Holy Ghost is come upon you: and ye shall be witnesses unto me, both in Jerusalem, and in all Judaea, and in Samaria, and unto the uttermost part of the earth. (Acts 1:4-5, 8)

II.   THE PROMISES
PERSONALLY FULFILLED

1. And when the day of Pentecost was fully come, they [the disciples] were all with one accord in one place. And suddenly there came a sound from heaven as of a rushing mighty wind, and it filled all the house where they were sitting. And there appeared unto them cloven tongues like as of fire, and it sat upon each of them. And they were filled with the Holy Ghost, and began to speak with other tongues, as the Spirit gave them utterance.

Now when this was noised abroad, the multitude came together, and were confounded, because that

241

every man heard them speak in his own language. And they were all amazed and marvelled, saying one to another, Behold, are not all these which speak Galilaeans? . . . We do hear them speak in our tongues the wonderful works of God. And they were all amazed, and were in doubt, saying one to another, What meaneth this? Others mocking said, These men are full of new wine. (Acts 2:1-4, 6-7, 11-13)

2.   But Peter, standing up with the eleven, lifted up his voice, and said unto them, Ye men of Judaea, and all ye that dwell at Jerusalem, be this known unto you, and hearken to my words: For these are not drunken, as ye suppose, seeing it is but the third hour of the day.

But this is that which was spoken by the prophet Joel; And it shall come to pass in the last days saith God, I will pour out of my Spirit upon all flesh: and your sons and your daughters shall prophesy, and your young men shall see visions, and your old men shall dream dreams. And on my servants and on my handmaidens I will pour out in those days of my Spirit; and they shall prophesy. (Acts 2:14-18)

3.   Ye men of Israel, hear these words; Jesus of Nazareth, a man approved of God among you by miracles and wonders and signs, which God did by him in the midst of you, as ye yourselves also know: Him, being delivered by the determinate counsel and foreknowledge of God, ye have taken, and by wicked hands have crucified and slain. . . . This Jesus hath God raised up, whereof we all are witnesses. Therefore, being by the right hand of God exalted, and having received of the Father the promise of the Holy Ghost, he hath shed forth this, which ye now see and hear. (Acts 2:22-23, 32-33)

III.
THE PATTERN
FOR PERSONAL FULFILLMENT

1. Now when they heard this, they were pricked in their heart, and said unto Peter and to the rest of the apostles, Men and brethren, what shall we do? Then Peter said unto them, Repent, and be baptized every one of you in the name of Jesus Christ for the remission of sins, and ye shall receive the gift of the Holy Ghost. For the promise is unto you, and to your children, and to all that are afar off, even as many as the Lord our God shall call. . . . Then they that gladly received his word were baptized: and the same day there were added unto them about three thousand souls. (Acts 2:37-39, 41)

2. Then Philip went down to the city of Samaria, and preached Christ unto them. . . . But when they believed Philip preaching of the things concerning the kingdom of God, and the name of Jesus Christ, they were baptized, both men and women.
　　Now when the apostles which were at Jerusalem heard that Samaria had received the word of God, they sent unto them Peter and John: Who, when they were come down, prayed for them, that they might receive the Holy Ghost: (For as yet he was fallen upon none of them: only they were baptized in the name of the Lord Jesus.) Then laid they their hands on them, and they received the Holy Ghost. (Acts 8:5, 12, 14-17)

3. And Ananias went his way, and entered into the house; and putting his hands on him said, Brother Saul, the Lord, even Jesus, that appeared unto thee in the way as thou camest, hath sent me, that thou mightest receive thy sight, and be filled with the Holy Ghost. And immediately there fell from his eyes as it

243

had been scales: and he received sight forthwith, and arose, and was baptized. (Acts 9:17-18)

4.   And as Peter was coming in, Cornelius [a devout gentile centurion] met him, and fell down at his feet, and worshipped him. But Peter took him up, saying, Stand up; I myself also am a man. And as he talked with him, he went in, and found many that were come together. And he said unto them, Ye know how that it is an unlawful thing for a man that is a Jew to keep company, or come unto one of another nation; but God hath showed me that I should not call any man common or unclean.

Then Peter opened his mouth, and said, Of a truth I perceive that God is no respecter of persons: But in every nation he that feareth him, and worketh righteousness, is accepted with him. The word which God sent unto the children of Israel, preaching peace by Jesus Christ: (he is Lord of all:) That word, I say, ye know, which was published throughout all Judaea, and began from Galilee, after the baptism which John preached; How God anointed Jesus of Nazareth with the Holy Ghost and with power: who went about doing good, and healing all that were oppressed of the devil; for God was with him.

And we are witnesses of all things which he did both in the land of the Jews, and in Jerusalem; whom they slew and hanged on a tree: Him God raised up the third day, and shewed him openly; Not to all the people, but unto witnesses chosen before of God, even to us, who did eat and drink with him after he rose from the dead. And he commanded us to preach unto the people, and to testify that it is he which was ordained of God to be the Judge of the quick and the dead. To him give all the prophets witness, that through his name whosoever believeth in him shall receive remission of sins.

While Peter yet spake these words, the Holy Ghost fell on all them which heard the word. And they of the circumcision [Jews] which believed were astonished, as many as came with Peter, because that on the Gentiles also was poured out the gift of the Holy Ghost. For they heard them speak with tongues, and magnify God. Then answered Peter, Can any man forbid water, that these should not be baptized, which have received the Holy Ghost as well as we? And he commanded them to be baptized in the name of the Lord. Then prayed they him to tarry certain days. (Acts 10:25-28, 34-48)

5. And the apostles and [Jewish] brethren that were in Judaea heard that the Gentiles had also received the word of God. And when Peter was come up to Jerusalem, they that were of the circumcision contended with him, Saying, Thou wentest in to men uncircumcised, and didst eat with them.

But Peter rehearsed the matter from the beginning, and expounded it by order unto them, saying . . . And as I began to speak [to the Gentiles], the Holy Ghost fell on them, as on us at the beginning. Then remembered I the word of the Lord, how that he said, John indeed baptized with water; but ye shall be baptized with the Holy Ghost. Forasmuch then as God gave them the like gift as he did unto us, who believed on the Lord Jesus Christ; what was I, that I could withstand God? When they heard these things, they held their peace, and glorified God. . . . (Acts 11:1-4, 15-18)

6. And it came to pass, that, while Apollos was at Corinth, Paul having passed through the upper coasts came to Ephesus: and finding certain disciples, He

said unto them, Have ye received the Holy Ghost since ye believed? And they said unto him, We have not so much as heard whether there be any Holy Ghost. And he said unto them, Unto what then were ye baptized? And they said, Unto John's baptism. Then said Paul, John verily baptized with the baptism of repentance, saying unto the people, that they should believe on him which should come after him, that is, on Christ Jesus.

When they heard this, they were baptized in the name of the Lord Jesus. And when Paul had laid his hands upon them, the Holy Ghost came on them; and they spake with tongues and prophesied. And all the men were about twelve. (Acts 19:1-7)

IV.   PERSONALLY APPROPRIATED BY FAITH

1.   This only would I [Paul] learn of you, Received ye the Spirit by the works of the law, or by the hearing of faith?

That the blessing of Abraham might come on the Gentiles through Jesus Christ; that we might receive the promise of the Spirit through faith. (Gal. 3:2, 14)

2.   He that believeth on me [Jesus], as the scripture hath said, out of his belly shall flow rivers of living water. (But this spake he of the Spirit, which they that believe on him should receive; for the Holy Ghost was not yet given; because that Jesus was not yet glorified.) (John 7:38-39)

3.   And I [Jesus] say unto you, Ask, and it shall be given you; seek, and ye shall find; knock, and it shall be opened unto you. For everyone that asketh receiveth; and he that seeketh findeth; and to him that

knocketh, it shall be opened.

If a son shall ask bread of any of you that is a father, will he give him a stone? or if he ask a fish, will he for a fish give him a serpent? Or if he shall ask an egg, will he offer him a scorpion? If ye then, being evil, know how to give good gifts unto your children: how much more shall your heavenly Father give the Holy Spirit to them that ask him? (Luke 11:9-13)

V.   THE PRIVILEGE OF INSPIRED PRAYER AND PRAISE FOR PERSONAL DEVOTIONS

After my words they spake not again; and my speech dropped upon them. And they waited for me as for the rain; and they opened their mouths wide as for the latter rain. (Job 29:22-23)

2.   Open thy mouth wide, and I will fill it. (Ps. 81:10)

3.   For with stammering lips and another tongue will he speak to this people. To whom he said, This is the rest wherewith ye may cause the weary to rest; and this is the refreshing: yet they would not hear. (Isa. 28:11-12)

4.   And they were all filled with the Holy Ghost, and began to speak with other tongues, as the Spirit gave them utterance. (Acts 2:4)

5.   While Peter yet spake these words, the Holy Ghost fell on all them which heard the word. For they heard them speak with tongues, and magnify God. (Acts 10:44, 46)

6.   And when Paul had laid his hands upon them,

the Holy Ghost came on them; and they spake with tongues. (Acts 19:6)

7. And these signs shall follow them that believe; In my name shall they cast out devils; they shall speak with new tongues. (Mark 16:17)

8. I [Paul] thank my God, I speak with tongues more than ye all [in private devotions] . . . [For] He that speaketh in an unknown tongue edifieth himself . . . [and] verily givest thanks well . . . he that speaketh in an unknown tongue, speaketh not unto men, but unto God: for no man understandeth him; howbeit in the spirit he speaketh mysteries. . . . For if I pray in an unknown tongue, my spirit prayeth, but my understanding is unfruitful. (I Cor. 14:18, 4, 17, 2, 14)

9. The Spirit also helpeth our infirmities: for we know not what we should pray for as we ought: but the Spirit itself maketh intercession for us with groanings which cannot be uttered. And he that searcheth the hearts knoweth what is the mind of the Spirit, because he maketh intercession for the saints according to the will of God. (Rom. 8:26-27)

10. But ye, beloved, building up yourselves on your most holy faith, praying in the Holy Ghost. (Jude 20)

11. Praying always with all prayer and supplication in the Spirit, and watching therunto with all perseverance and supplication for all saints. (Eph. 6:18)

12. By him therefore let us offer the sacrifice of praise to God continually, that is, the fruit of our lips giving thanks to his name. (Heb. 13:15)

13. Let my prayer be set forth before thee as incense: and the lifting up of my hands as the evening sacrifice. (Ps. 141:2)

14. O magnify the Lord with me, and let us exalt his name together. (Ps. 34:3)

15. I will bless the Lord at all times: his praise shall continually be in my mouth. (Ps. 34:1)

VI. MARKS OF THE SPIRIT-FILLED CHRISTIAN

And they were all *filled* with the Holy Ghost, and began to speak with other tongues, as the Spirit gave them utterance. (Acts 2:4)

2. And now, Lord, behold their threatenings: and grant unto thy servants, that with all boldness they may speak thy word, By stretching forth thine hand to heal; and that signs and wonders may be done by the name of thy holy child Jesus.

And when they had prayed, the place was shaken where they were assembled together; and they were *filled* with the Holy Ghost, and they spake the word of God with boldness. (Acts 4:29-31)

3. Wherefore, brethren, look ye out among you seven men of honest report, *full* of the Holy Ghost and wisdom, whom we may appoint over this business. (Acts 6:3)

4. And the saying pleased the whole multitude: and they chose Stephen, a man *full* of faith and of the Holy Ghost . . . And Stephen, full of faith and power, did great wonders and miracles among the people. (Acts 6:5,8)

5.   And the disciples were *filled* with joy, and with the Holy Ghost. (Acts 13:52)

6.   Now the God of hope *fill* you with all joy and peace in believing, that ye may abound in hope, through the power of the Holy Ghost. (Rom. 15:13)

7.   And be not drunk with wine, wherein is excess; but be *filled* with the Spirit; Speaking to yourselves in psalms and hymns and spiritual songs, singing and making melody in your heart to the Lord: Giving thanks always for all things unto God and the Father in the name of our Lord Jesus Christ. (Eph. 5:18-20)